TOCQUEVILLE'S CIVIL RELIGION

SUNY SERIES IN RELIGION, CULTURE, AND SOCIETY
WADE CLARK ROOF, EDITOR

TOCQUEVILLE'S CIVIL RELIGION

AMERICAN CHRISTIANITY
AND THE
PROSPECTS FOR FREEDOM

Sanford Kessler

STATE UNIVERSITY OF NEW YORK PRESS

Published by
State University of New York Press, Albany

For information, address State University of New York
Press, State University Plaza, Albany, N.Y., 12246

Production by Diane Ganeles
Marketing by Bernadette LaManna

Library of Congress Cataloging-in-Publication Data

Kessler, Sanford, 1945–
    Tocqueville's civil religion : American Christianity and the
prospects for freedom / Sanford Kessler.
        p.   cm.—(SUNY series in religion, culture, and society)
    Includes bibliographical references and index.
    ISBN 0-7914-1929-0 (CH : alk. paper).—ISBN 0-7914-1930-4 (PB :
alk. paper)
        1. Civil religion—United States—History—19th century.
    2. Tocqueville, Alexis de, 1805–1859. De la démocratie en Amérique.
    3. United States—Church history—19th century.   4. Christianity and
politics.   5. Democracy—Religious aspects—Christianity.
    I. Title. II. Series
    BR525.K47   1994
    277.3'08'092—dc20   93-26778
                                                                        CIP

10 9 8 7 6 5 4 3 2 1

FOR SHEVA

CONTENTS

PREFACE

My concern with the relationship between biblical religion and American democracy, the subject of this book, derives from personal experiences as a Jewish child growing up amidst the conflicting demands of traditional Jewish observance and American secularism. In later years, when pondering my own stance toward Judaism, I often wondered why religious orthodoxy appealed so little to mid-century American Jews. Tocqueville's perceptive and subtle analysis of how modern democracy undermines faith provided the explanation I sought. Although Tocqueville said little about Judaism, his observations on American Christianity shed light on the way modernity affects all biblical religions. His description of how American Christians tailored traditional religious morality to democracy's secular propensities, for example, surely applied, and continues to apply to the vast majority of American Jews. Most of us, like our Christian counterparts, rely on private judgment rather than the Bible when making moral decisions.

Having come of age in the sixties, I witnessed and participated in the general questioning of authority that further eroded the influence of faith. Tocqueville's insights into the American mind helped me to understand this massive assault on tradition and the ensuing moral revolution. The sixties generation sought to increase equality and freedom, two of our nation's core principles. In accomplishing this aim, it achieved greater justice for women and blacks, created new opportunities for personal development, and fostered a significant amount of short-term and long-term idealism. At the same time, however, it bolstered selfish materialism and weakened family, social, and political ties. These latter trends have altered our national character in politically harmful ways. Although America is now relatively free from external military threat, its internal moral decay is both obvious and ominous.

Tocqueville convinced me that thoughtful Americans who cherish self-government must consider a political role for religion in addressing our country's moral ills. He deemed religion important for character building, especially where a country's spiritual resources are endangered. Thus, he designed a "reasonable" form of Christianity to replace the traditional versions of the faith that he considered hostile to and threatened by democratic freedom. This Christianity, which I refer to in my book as a civil religion, strongly resembles the dominant forms of American Christianity in Tocqueville's day and in our own.

Tocqueville's emphasis on the utility of religion and, more broadly, on how good morals strengthen freedom, made him, as he put it, a "liberal of a new kind" (Tocqueville 1860–1866, 5:431; my translation).[1] Most liberal thinkers today consider religion and morality outside the realm of public policy and are largely unfamiliar with his work. Recent critics of American liberalism cite this relative indifference to character as one of its fatal flaws. The most politically potent of these are the religious fundamentalists whose numbers and strength have grown dramatically in recent years. Such challenges touch a raw nerve among some liberals, provoking them to look within their own tradition for lessons on how to improve character.

Tocqueville's *Democracy in America* provides just such guidance, offering the most brilliant and searching account of America ever written. The *Democracy* treats America's national character comprehensively, relating it to our unique history, our democratic social condition, and our remarkable historical success in maintaining freedom. Tocqueville thus offers a rich and surprisingly timely perspective to statesmen and citizens grappling with our multifaceted moral crisis.

Others, too, beyond American shores may benefit from Tocqueville's work. I began this preface in Moscow where a new Russian translation of the *Democracy* now circulates along with other less attractive manifestations of Western culture. In the 1830s, Tocqueville was quite pessimistic about Russia's future, believing the country was somehow fated to live under despotism. Such was the case for about a century and a half after he made this dire prediction. Yet Russia now struggles bravely against nightmarish odds to secure free institutions for its long-suffering people. I hope the *Democracy*, which Tocqueville wrote for fledgling democrats, can assist them in this task.

My book focuses on Tocqueville's religious-political thought as it appears in the *Democracy* and in his other writings and correspondence. Following Tocqueville's advice, I treat this aspect of his work as central to his analysis of freedom's moral requirements and of the tasks of statesmanship. In explicating Tocqueville's ideas and bringing them to bear on current problems, I wish to contribute in some small way to strengthening freedom both in America and abroad.

I also hope to do justice to Tocqueville's noble spirit, a spirit I have lived with constantly for the past several years.

ACKNOWLEDGMENTS

I would first like to acknowledge those readers who helped me to complete this book and to absolve them of blame for its flaws. Thanks to: Ruth W. Grant of Duke University, who scrutinized all parts of this work as it developed with a kind and discerning eye; Marvin Meyers, my mentor, who kindled my love for Tocqueville and for America during my undergraduate years at Brandeis University; Robert K. Faulkner, my dissertation adviser at Boston College and now a cherished colleague and friend; Ernst M. Manasse, a true philosopher whose gentle but probing voice challenged my thinking in important respects; Wilson Carey McWilliams of Rutgers University and Wade Clark Roof of the University of California at Santa Barbara, who reviewed my manuscript for SUNY Press and made generous and insightful comments; and the following friends who helped in small, but important ways: Elias Baumgarten of the University of Michigan at Dearborn; Romand Coles and Kimberly Curtis of Duke University; Joshua Miller of Lafayette College; and Carmine A. Prioli of North Carolina State University.

I also wish to thank the National Endowment for the Humanities and the Earhart Foundation for generous and much appreciated financial support; North Carolina State University and its Department of Political Science and Public Administration for the released time that made this study possible; also Rosalie L. Robertson, Christine Worden, and Diane Ganeles of SUNY Press for their patience and cheerful assistance; Caroline Benforado and the late Erika Fairchild of North Carolina State University for aid with translations; and especially William H. Friedman for invaluable personal support and help with writing.

Finally, thanks to the members of my long-suffering family for their goodwill and support in what seemed to be, and in fact was, a never-ending process: my mother Sarah Kessler and sister Trudie Kessler, for giving encouragement from afar; my daughter Benna Kessler, for constantly reminding me that life extends beyond this book; and my wife Sheva Zucker, to whom this work is dedicated, for her endless good humor and love.

• • •

Portions of this work appeared in different form over the past several years in *The Journal of Politics, Polity, Interpretation, Journal of Church and State,* and *Tocqueville's Defense of Human Liberty: Current Essays* edited by Peter Augustine Lawler and Joseph Alulis (New York and London: Garland Publishing Company, 1993).

CHAPTER ONE

INTRODUCTION

Despotism may be able to do without faith, but freedom cannot . . . How could society escape destruction if, when political ties are relaxed, moral ties are not tightened? And what can be done with a people master of itself if it is not subject to God? (294)[1]

The French political philosopher Alexis de Tocqueville was the greatest thinker to ponder the complex relationship between modern democracy, religion, and freedom. Tocqueville wrote during an era in which post-revolutionary France was making a bumpy and politically painful transition from aristocracy to democracy. A fierce battle between liberals and traditionalists regarding the merits of religion was then in progress, perpetuating the great rifts in society caused by the Revolution (15–18). Tocqueville expended considerable energy attempting to reconcile these two groups. The "spectacle" of their disunion, he lamented near the end of his life, "has weighed on my soul and oppressed it. . . . I feel this today as sharply as I did when young." No thought "has been more present to my mind" (Tocqueville 1951–, 15(2): 206; my translation).

1

Tocqueville went to America with his friend Gustave de Beaumont in 1830 ostensibly to study the American prison system, but with the deeper purpose of "examining in detail and as scientifically as possible" all elements of American life (cited in Schleifer 1980, 3; Tocqueville 1860–1866, 5:412). He discovered shortly after his arrival that American religion supported freedom and was universally respected. Believing as he did that French liberals and traditionalists could both learn from America's example, he spent considerable time observing American religion on his journey and later placing his empirical observations in a broad theoretical framework.[2]

My main object in this book is to understand what Tocqueville learned from these efforts. How, for example, did he perceive the relationship between American democracy and Christianity? Did he consider this relationship troubled or harmonious? What factors, in his view, affected American Christianity's development and what was this religion's role in shaping our national character? What exactly did Tocqueville mean by calling religion the "first" of America's political institutions while praising religious disestablishment (292, 295)? Finally, if Christianity is essential to democratic freedom as Tocqueville suggests, how relevant to contemporary America are his recommendations for strengthening it?

Despite Tocqueville's acknowledged preeminence in American studies, most scholars mention him only in passing, if at all, when dealing with religion's role in American life (see, for example, Carter 1993).[3] Those Tocquevillians who have treated his religious-political thought extensively have not related this thought to current issues. These are regrettable omissions. Although Tocqueville studied American religion with nineteenth-century Europeans in mind, his views on this subject may well be useful to us. He is the only great political philosopher to deal comprehensively with the origin, development, character, and political significance of our country's predominant faith. Given his remarkable foresight, it should not surprise us if his thoughts on this subject shed considerable light on today's political problems.

Unfortunately, these problems abound. Americans in the twilight years of the twentieth century are enjoying little of the buoyant optimism which marked the end of the nineteenth century and even less of our revolutionary generation's sober self-confidence. There is a certain irony in this, since the liberal democratic principles which sparked the American revolution have recently triumphed over Marxism-Leninism just as they helped vanquish fascism and Naziism almost fifty years ago. Our victory in the Cold War signals the end of the only remaining theoretically grounded and globally based challenge to American principles.

Although this victory is a just cause for celebration and pride, a host of grave domestic problems have tarnished its lustre and seriously compromised our political health. The most visible of these are corruption in government, racial conflict, hardcore poverty, broken families, violent crime, and rampant drug use (see Bennett 1993).[4] Less visible, but more serious, are the spiritual ills which impoverish our private and public lives. Although strong and prosperous as a nation, we seem less able as individuals to enjoy the personal satisfactions promised by our principles. We have also lost much of the trust, mutual respect, and sense of shared values which enable countries to weather unsettling social change and political controversy (Bellah et al. 1991, 3–4; Galston 1991, 6).

Much of the harshness of contemporary American politics may be attributed to an ongoing "culture war" which touches the lives of us all. The frontline battles in this war involve policy matters such as abortion, welfare, health care, prayer in the public schools, affirmative action, and gay rights. As James Davison Hunter points out, however, these battles are mere skirmishes in a deeper conflict over different moral and metaphysical principles. At the heart of this conflict is a question of ultimate authority: What guide should we use to determine what is good and bad, true and untrue (Hunter 1991, 34, 42, 49, 119)?

Now, as in Tocqueville's time, traditionalists and liberals are adversaries (Hunter 1991, 46).[5] Traditionalists blame the bulk of our problems on the moral failings of the American people and believe that only respect for an "external, definable, and transcendent" moral authority will restore our psychological and political health (Hunter 1991, 44). For most, this means allegiance to some form of biblical orthodoxy. The bulk of politically active traditionalists today are Protestant evangelicals. Their allies often include conservative Catholics and orthodox Jews whose sympathy with their moral commitments outweighs their antipathy toward fundamentalist theology (Hunter 1991, 45–47).

Liberals hold that private, rational judgment is the only final authority consistent with American principles and the best guide to happiness and truth. They blame our assorted ills on the inability of American political institutions to respond democratically to pressing economic and social needs, and would popularize government, expand individual rights, and above all, reduce economic inequality (Hunter 1991, 113–115). Liberals are generally skeptical of all orthodoxies and consider moral and religious diversity a positive good. Their numbers include avowed secularists as well as Christians, Jews, and Muslims who choose their own level of religious observance on the basis of personal experience and inclination (Hunter 1991, 45).

In recent years, a third, less powerful group, whose members I shall call religious functionalists, has sought to bridge the gap between these bitter opponents. Religious functionalists are liberals who think religion necessary to foster the mores that sustain freedom.[6] In this respect, they differ from traditionalists who define freedom as righteous living, and from most of their fellow liberals who downplay the link between character and freedom's survival. They are an eclectic bunch, less connected to broad national constituencies than the other two groups, and more difficult to categorize in terms of their overall political and religious views. Some write as Christians who believe that Christian theology supports the principles of liberal democracy. Others, more reticent about their private beliefs, argue the political merits of Christianity strictly on utilitarian grounds.[7]

America's culture war is currently being fought on many fronts—the family, the churches, the schools and universities, the law, electoral politics, and, most important, the court of public opinion (Hunter 1991, 51). Here activists compete, using the weapons of modern technology to pull middle America toward their distinctive moral visions (Hunter 1991, 34, 43, 48). Victory in this competition brings with it the power to shape the "public culture" which orders our lives as citizens (Hunter 1991, 54). This accounts in part for the struggle's peculiar intensity and seeming intractability. At stake, as Hunter points out, is "*the meaning of America*, (his emphasis) who we have been in the past, who we are now, and perhaps most important, who we, as a nation, will aspire to become in the new millenium" (Hunter 1991, 50).

In this study, I analyze and critique Tocqueville's views on some key issues related to this conflict. The first concerns the role of Christianity in the American founding; the second, the strength and nature of American Christianity today; and the third, the proper role of religion in a free society. I shall call these respectively the historical, the sociological, and the political dimensions of Tocqueville's understanding of American faith.

Needless to say, scholarly controversies surround all three issues. Although my primary goal in studying Tocqueville is to elucidate his thought, I also hope to contribute a Tocquevillian perspective to these disputes. In the rest of this chapter I shall discuss the various points of contention, briefly summarize Tocqueville's position on them, and orient the reader to the chapters to come.

Before proceeding to these matters, however, I must briefly address some preliminary problems relating to the nature and scope of my subject. Tocqueville was a practicing, if not a believing Catholic, and was highly pleased with the Catholic presence in Jacksonian America. His particular focus in *Democracy in America*, however, was on Protestantism, as mine will be in this analysis. Tocqueville believed that American religious mores were and would always be predominantly Protestant (288–290, 435, 640–642). Modern analysts tend to agree despite the fact that America has become much more religiously diverse since Tocqueville wrote. As George Kelly put it:

> Although Roman Catholics are, by far, our largest single church . . . few who have lived their lives in the United States would doubt that dissenting Protestantism is the wellspring of our ethos. Despite distinctive Catholic and Jewish contributions to our political, professional, and intellectual life, America is most plausibly to be examined as a land of the avatars and the pathology of Protestantism (Kelly 1983, 207).

In this book, I shall frequently use the term "civil religion" when referring to American Christianity. Since this usage is currently controversial, a few words about its appropriateness are in order. If religion may roughly be defined as a means through which human beings recognize and revere God, civil religion refers to a religion (or elements of religious belief and practice) which purports to be theocentric, but in fact is designed to serve secular, as opposed to transcendent or otherworldly ends. In 1967, Robert N. Bellah ignited a flurry of interest in civil religion by arguing that such a faith has existed in America since the early days of the Republic (Bellah 1974).[8] Although he originally used the term to describe a nonsectarian creed which placed America in a theological framework (Bellah 1974, 29), he, as well as others, has referred to aspects of American Christianity itself as a civil religion (Bellah 1976, 57; Rouner 1986, 128; Zuckert 1986, 181–203).[9]

In the past few years, most participants in this debate have rejected the term "civil religion" for a variety of reasons.[10] Some consider the idea of civil religion distasteful, if not politically dangerous, because the word "civil" conjures up an uncritical worship of America and her values (Moltmann 1986, 41–58). Although Bellah dissociated his use of the term from any simple patriotism or statism, he ultimately abandoned it because of these definitional controversies which, in his view, drew attention away from more substantive issues (Bellah 1989, 147).

Others see the term as an academic construct with little or no correspondence to American reality. They believe that the vast majority of Americans are traditional, God-fearing Christians who view civil religion, as Richard John Neuhaus put it, "as a threat to be resisted rather than a benefit to be embraced" (Neuhaus 1986, 103). While these scholars agree that a large number of Americans do share certain theological beliefs about their country, they consider these beliefs an integral part of American Christianity or a Christian component of a national public philosophy (Mathisen 1989, 134; Neuhaus 1986, 99, 103–109; Wilson 1986, 111–123 esp. 122).

Many of these critics also object to the idea of Christianity as a civil religion strictly on definitional grounds. There are many versions of traditional Christianity, both Catholic and Protestant, which differ from each other theologically and ecclesiastically. All of these, however, are theocentric, universal faiths that require belief in the supernatural and obedience to an external moral authority. Their chief purpose is to help human beings attain salvation rather than to strengthen or legitimate political orders, and their attachments to these orders are always subordinate and conditional. Indeed, giving primacy to earthly things at the expense of faith is considered idolatry, the primary evil in the biblical canon. Thus, to refer to these types of Christianity as civil religions, the argument goes, grossly misrepresents them. If, on the other hand, a refashioned version of Christianity no longer serves transcendent, transnational ends, it may be a civil religion, but it is not a genuine biblical faith (Herberg 1974, 86–87; Neuhaus 1986, 101–103).

These criticisms have some validity. To speak of American Christianity only as a civil religion is unjust to the faith and to the self-understanding of many Americans. It also oversimplifies, reducing a multifaceted phenomenon to one of its more salient parts. We shall therefore not equate the two. Instead, we shall use the term "civil religion" to refer to mainline Christianity, which Wade Clark Roof defines as "the dominant, culturally established religious faiths that are closely associated with prevailing social values and mores" (Roof 1983, 131). This excludes Protestant evangelicalism from the category as well as the conservative, Rome-oriented branch of American Catholicism. It does include, however, the vast majority of American churches today as well as the vast majority of American churches Tocqueville observed and admired.[11]

As Tocqueville will show us, mainline Christianity was and is qualitatively different from traditional Christianity in important respects. The key difference concerns the locus of moral authority. In contrast to the traditional faiths, our mainline faiths, for the most part, make the individual, rather than divine revelation, the ultimate arbiter of duty and truth. This shift makes them more anthropocentric than theocentric, and more compatible with secular than with biblical morality. Historically, these faiths strengthened our national character, contributed to our economic prosperity, and muted religious conflict in ways that traditional Christianity could never do. Although mainline American Christianity was originally otherworldly and theocentric, by Tocqueville's time it had been "civilized" in ways that made these political accomplishments possible. And it was no longer a genuine biblical faith.

RELIGION AND THE AMERICAN FOUNDING

Serious attempts to understand our nation's history usually start by examining our origins because, as most Americanists would agree, our founding decisively shaped our regime. The majority of these scholars trace our beginnings to a philosophical rather than to a religious tradition and point most frequently to the British philosopher John Locke as America's intellectual forebear.[12] According to this view, Locke's political thought as it appears in his *Two Treatises on Government* and *A Letter on Toleration* greatly influenced Thomas Jefferson and the Framers of the Constitution.

Jefferson set forth America's basic political principles in the Declaration of Independence, and the "Bill for Establishing Religious Freedom," so the argument goes, building on the idea that all human beings have an equal natural right to freedom. The Framers established a representative democracy based on these principles and designed the Constitution to protect freedom by fragmenting political and social power. With the adoption of the First Amendment, they formally relegated religion to the private sphere, thereby forever preventing it from hindering their secular aims.

In recent years, a growing number of scholars have maintained that Christianity had the greatest influence on our founding. Some of these argue that the Framers themselves were religious and that their piety influenced their work.[13] Others, however, contend that the Puritans founded America by establishing biblical principles as the basis of our political life.[14] In their view, the most important of these principles was the idea of the covenant, or a communal agreement sanctioned by God. Puritan covenants, they maintain, were the major theoretical sources for American constitutionalism, shaping both our political institutions and our national character in a variety of ways.[15]

THE SECULARIZATION DEBATE

The scholarly dispute over the nature, strength, and direction of American religion today is generally known as the "secularization debate." Peter L. Berger defines secularization as the "process by which sectors of society and culture are removed from the domination of religious institutions and symbols" (Berger 1967, 106). Those who believe that America has gradually become more secular give a variety of explanations which are not always mutually exclusive. Some contend that the

forces of modernity (e.g., science, technology, indus-
trialization, and urbanization) are incompatible with
biblical religion, and that America as the vanguard
modern nation cannot sustain a vital Christian faith.
A Marxist version of this argument holds that Christianity is a capitalist tool of oppression destined for
oblivion as the masses become more politically aware
(Wald 1987, 3–6). Finally, others believe that secularization resulted from the spread of enlightenment philosophy at the expense of biblical faith (Kristol 1991,
22).

Dissenters from this view generally fall into two
groups. The first concedes that America has recently
become more irreligious, but argues that this trend is
neither as irreversible nor as pervasive as it once appeared (Berger 1983, 14). The second group, believing
secularization a figment of the academic imagination,
cites empirical evidence to show that Americans have
been consistently religious at least since the early 1920s
(Caplow et al. 1983, 36, 280; Gallup and Castelli 1989,
4; Greeley 1989 8, 116, 128; Wald 1987 7–10). As
Neuhaus put it, "the democratic reality, even, if you
will, the raw demographic reality, is that most Americans derive their values and visions from the biblical
tradition" (Neuhaus 1984, 139).

A recent scientific study of American public opinion
appears to support this contention. In their book, *The
People's Religion: American Faith in the 90's*, George
Gallup, Jr. and Jim Castelli report that over 90 percent
of all Americans believe in God, 88 percent never
doubted His existence, and 90 percent pray; 80 percent
believe in miracles and divine reward and punishment;
and a large majority claim church membership, believe
in life after death, and respect the religious authority of
the Bible, deeming it the literal or inspired word of God
(Gallup and Castelli 1989, 4, 16, 45, 56, 60).

Data such as this has led Gallup and Castelli to conclude that the "degree of religious orthodoxy found among Americans is simply amazing." They continue:

> A country in which such large proportions of the population believe in a personal God who will call them to Judgment Day to determine how they spend the afterlife; in which so many believe that God has a plan for their lives and communicates with them; in which one-third report intense, life-changing religious experiences; in which so many worship Jesus Christ—such a nation cannot by any stretch of the imagination be described as secular in its core beliefs (Gallup and Castelli 1989, 90).

The "core beliefs" that shape a nation's character are, as Gallup and Castelli suggest, those opinions about God, human nature, the meaning of life, and the afterlife that form the basis of almost every human action. If America's core beliefs are truly orthodox, that is if they derive from traditional Christianity, then Gallup and Castelli's evidence would seem to discredit the secularization theory.

There is other evidence in *The People's Religion*, however, which supports the proponents of this theory. We learn in the book, for example, that American religiosity though widespread, is largely superficial. It does not deeply affect the mores of most Americans, who tend to follow their own independent judgment rather than religious authority when dealing with life's problems. Moreover, a large number of nominal Christians neither attend church nor participate actively in congregational affairs. Finally, only a small number of Americans read the Bible frequently, or possess even the most rudimentary knowledge of their faith:

> Fewer than half of all adults can name Matthew, Mark, Luke and John as the four Gospels of the New Testament, while many do not know that Jesus had twelve

disciples or that he was born in Bethlehem. In addition, a large majority of Americans believe that the Ten Commandments are still valid rules for living today, but they have a tough time recalling exactly what those rules are (Gallup and Castelli 1989 60, 21, 69, 90).

Gallup and Castelli fail to resolve this paradox, perhaps because they haven't sufficiently reflected on the nature of Christian orthodoxy. Virtually all forms of traditional Christianity require believers to know and to understand the central tenets of their faith, to submit unconditionally to God's will as revealed in Scripture, and to act on the basis of their religious commitments (Tipton 1983, 81, 82). If American Christians fail to meet these requirements, their degree of orthodoxy may be "simply amazing" but not in the way these writers suggest.

RELIGION AND AMERICAN POLITICAL LIFE

Protestant evangelicals believe, as did their Puritan ancestors, that America's founding was divinely inspired and that the Bible should ultimately rule our political life (Hunter 1991, 109–113). Some evangelicals reject religious disestablishment altogether in favor of a theocratic model of government based on Old Testament law (Hunter 1991, 262). Theocracy, they hope, will rid America of her present corruption and make her the moving force in a worldwide Christian revival (Wuthnow 1988, 396). More mainstream evangelicals would merely strengthen America's national character by selecting "godly" leadership and legalizing certain elements of biblical morality (Hunter 1991, 8, 112). Their model for American church–state relations is the informal establishment of Protestantism that existed in this country throughout most of the nineteenth century (Neuhaus 1984, 93).

Liberals have dominated the American church–state debate for the past several decades, although their power has waned considerably in recent years. In addition to arguing for a secular founding, they oppose all public aid to religion, no matter how general, on the grounds that it violates the rights of the irreligious. This "strict separationist" position currently informs the Supreme Court's interpretation of the First Amendment's Establishment Clause. The state, according to this view, "can do nothing which involves governmental support of religion or which is favorable to the cultivation of religious interests" (cited in O'Brien 1991, 644). Although some strict separationists defend this principle on religious grounds, most view it as the best means for ridding public life of all Christian influence (Neuhaus 1992, 13–17).

As we have seen, religious functionalists take a middle position, arguing that while America's ultimate purpose is to promote freedom, religion is a vital means to this end. I shall set forth their general argument in some detail because, as we shall see, it comes closest to approximating Tocqueville's view of religion's proper political role. The nerve of this argument is that only religion can foster the mores needed to insure that free institutions function properly. These include the character-strengthening virtues which indirectly guard freedom as well as certain beliefs regarding the sanctity of rights which protect freedom directly. Religion, according to this argument, also gives freedom a positive dimension reminding us of our social duties and our spiritual needs. Finally, it teaches that the poor, the marginal, and the vulnerable require protection and respect (see Neuhaus, 1984, 21, 75–76, 92–93, 118, 140).

Although religious functionalists disagree over the extent to which Christianity informed our founding, most view the late eighteenth-century Founders as allies in their fight to legitimize a political role for American religion today. Thus their writings often contain classic statements by these men that link America's political health to widespread religious belief (see, for example, Galston 1991, 264).

One of the most frequently cited of these appears in George Washington's Farewell Address. "Of all the dispositions and habits which lead to political prosperity," Washington (or Hamilton) wrote, "Religion and morality are indispensable supports. . . . 'Tis substantially true that virtue or morality is a necessary spring of popular government" (Washington 1940, 229). Another favorite is a famous passage from Thomas Jefferson's *Notes on the State of Virginia*. Despite his skepticism toward revealed religion, Jefferson wrote that the only security for the "liberties of a nation" is "a conviction in the minds of the people that these liberties are of the gift of God" (Jefferson 1944, 278).

Richard John Neuhaus makes a strong contemporary argument for religious functionalism in his recent book, *The Naked Public Square*. Neuhaus links America's moral–political crisis to fundamentalist and liberal errors regarding the proper role of religion in our public life. His first quarrel is with those Protestant evangelicals who would impose their faith on the country at large. Neuhaus strongly opposes their irrationality, their intolerance, and their authoritarian theological claims. "Whatever may be the alternatives to secularistic views of American society," he writes, "they cannot be permitted to violate the imperatives of pluralism or to undo the great constitutional achievement represented by the 'free exercise' and 'no establishment' clauses of the First Amendment" (Neuhaus 1984, 8, 36–37, 52; Neuhaus 1986, 107).

Neuhaus' chief adversaries, though, are the liberals who would remove religion entirely from our public life. Their goal, as he interprets it, is to establish a "naked

public square" where policies are discussed and imple-
mented without reference to faith. Neuhaus thinks this
goal is chimerical because, in the last analysis, policy
is always based on "moral judgments of an ultimate
nature" (Neuhaus 1984, 82). Rather than cleansing
American politics of faith, today's liberals, he maintains, have merely replaced its Christian foundations
with secular humanism, an *ersatz* religion which strips
life of transcendent meaning. According to Neuhaus,
secular humanism has contributed significantly to our
current moral crisis by detaching the public understanding of freedom from its traditional religious restraints. Its long-term tendency is to promote
totalitarianism, both by removing religion as a check to
the state's ambitions and by creating a spiritual void
which feeds these ambitions (Neuhaus 1984, 24–25,
80, 82, 86–87; see also Carter 1993, 34–39, 51–56).

Neuhaus wants to restore religion to its once prominent instrumental role in American public life. His first
goal is to engage American churches and synagogues
in a dialogue which would reconstruct a national public philosophy based on our common religious values.
This public philosophy would be rationally defensible
and inclusive despite its particularistic religious roots
(Neuhaus 1986, 98–110, esp. 105–109). His second goal
is to reinstitute the non-preferential government support and encouragement for religion which existed for
most of our history. Thus, he backs a variety of policies
currently proscribed by the Supreme Court including
government aid to religious education and the display
of religious symbols in public places (Neuhaus 1984,
148, 152; Neuhaus 1990, 64–65; Neuhaus 1992, 13–
18).

Neuhaus talks mostly about the public rather than
the private dimensions of American religiosity because
he thinks that the religious mores of the American people

are orthodox and strong (Neuhaus 1984, 113). In this respect, he parts company with other religious functionalists who accept the secularization theory (see, for example, Kristol 1991).[16] This issue of Christianity's popular strength is obviously of great concern to all parties interested in defining religion's public role. If popular Christianity is weak, those favoring such a role must revitalize it before all else, while those opposing it need only stay the course. If popular Christianity is strong, however, the first group can focus on changing public policy as Neuhaus suggests, while the second group must redouble its efforts at popular enlightenment.

TOCQUEVILLE'S VIEWS

Tocqueville considered the Puritans America's founders, thereby supporting those scholars who claim that Christianity decisively influenced the nature of our regime. His case for a Puritan founding rests on the premise that the Puritans shaped our national character and that character is more vital than even the best written constitution to the maintenance of freedom.

While Tocqueville regarded America as the most Christian country in the world in the 1830s, he was an early proponent of the secularization theory, at least as it applies to the West. Tocqueville considered democracy responsible for secularization as well as for modernization and the spread of enlightenment philosophy. Although he occasionally suggested that democracy is hospitable to biblical faith, that Christianity is wholly democratic in principle, and that God himself set the democratic revolution in motion, his final judgment was that equality had a corrosive effect on religion. While he admired American Christianity, he concluded that religion had less influence on America's national character in the 1830s than certain secular moral principles based on self-interest.

This judgment made Tocqueville quite guarded about the future of American Christianity and its long-term ability to contribute to our country's political health. In the end he feared that democratic skepticism would deepen the widespread doubt and indifference already visible in the 1830s and would lead Americans to embrace materialist philosophies hostile to freedom.

Tocqueville wrote *Democracy in America* in part to teach democratic statesmen and moralists how to make religion serve the cause of freedom in a predominantly secular age. His emphasis on religion's political importance made him a religious functionalist or as he called himself, a "liberal of a new kind" (Tocqueville 1860–1866, 5: 431; my translation). As a liberal, he opposed all forms of biblical orthodoxy, considering them hostile in principle to freedom. He also, however, rejected the prevailing liberal view that free, democratic societies can easily survive without some type of widespread religious belief.

Although a practicing Catholic, Tocqueville was part of a French philosophical tradition that sought to replace traditional Christianity with a freedom-oriented civil religion. Building on the thought of Montesquieu and Rousseau, Tocqueville developed a reasonable form of Christianity which he considered more suitable for modern democracy than the prevailing orthodoxies. Tocqueville believed that America of the 1830s had already incorporated certain elements of this civil creed into its mores and that America's religious political arrangements could serve in important respects as a model for France.

At the same time, however, he prepared his readers for a future in which Christianity might be too weak to be politically useful. To this end he set forth a multifaceted secular strategy for preserving freedom which complemented his argument for civil religion.

The next three chapters of this book set forth the theoretical framework within which Tocqueville makes his case. Chapter 2 discusses Tocqueville's overall approach to religion, focusing on his personal religious beliefs, their bearing on his political thought, and his stature as a political philosopher. Chapter 3 examines Tocqueville's civil version of Christianity in detail, paying special attention to its democratic components and its intellectual roots. Chapter 4 explores Tocqueville's views on how statesmen can use religion to promote freedom and why French statesmen failed in this regard.

Chapters 5 through 8 deal directly with Tocqueville's thoughts on American religion and politics. Chapter 5 discusses his analysis of America's Puritan founding and the various factors that transformed traditional American Protestantism into a civil religion. Chapter 6 discusses Tocqueville's understanding of how democracy threatens freedom and how religion protected it in Jacksonian America. Chapter 7 examines the weaknesses of American religion during this time and what it consequently failed to do for the cause of freedom. Chapter 8 discusses the grounds for Tocqueville's pessimism regarding American religion's future and the tasks he sets for American statesmen and moralists in light of this pessimism.

Chapter 9 evaluates Tocqueville's overall analysis, paying special attention to those parts which bear on our current moral–political difficulties. I argue that despite its flaws, this analysis is an indispensable guide to understanding and addressing these difficulties. I conclude by suggesting that popular belief in a "civil" version of Christianity properly attuned to current needs can better serve the cause of freedom than either widespread religious orthodoxy or the widespread absence of faith.

CHAPTER TWO

TOCQUEVILLE'S APPROACH TO RELIGION

*Though it is very important for man as an individual
that his religion should be true, that is not the case
for society. Society has nothing to fear or hope from
another life; what is most important for it is not that
all citizens should profess the true religion but that
they should profess religion (290).*

Tocqueville's analysis of American Christianity was
part of a bold attempt to formulate a new relationship
between religion and politics for his native France and,
more broadly, for all modern free democracies. To understand and to assess this relationship properly, we
must first identify its metaphysical roots. Was
Tocqueville a believing Christian or a skeptic, and how
did his attitude toward faith affect his politics? Did his
first principles limit or enhance the quality and current
relevance of his thought?

The first point at issue concerns the bearing of
Tocqueville's personal faith or lack of it on his religious–political views. "However sincere a Christian
Tocqueville himself may have been," Marvin Zetterbaum
writes, "he conceived of *Democracy in America* as a political treatise; and in it, as in all his political writings,

21

he considers religion with an eye to its political utility"
(Zetterbaum 1967). Indeed, Tocqueville lends credence
to this view by suggesting that a social scientist can
sidestep the issue of religion's truth. "Though it is very
important for man as an individual that his religion
should be true," he maintained in the *Democracy*, "that
is not the case for society. Society has nothing to fear
or hope from another life" (290).

As Ralph C. Hancock points out, however, such
remarks do not allow us simply to ignore the question
of Tocqueville's piety. Ultimately, perceptions of political utility are based on a metaphysically grounded view
of human nature (Hancock 1991, 351–352). Tocqueville,
of course, was aware of this fact. The "common spring"
for all human judgments as well as actions, he observed, is the "very general conception men have of
God, of His relations with the human race, of the nature of their soul, and of their duties to their fellows"
(442–443). If this observation is correct, Tocqueville's
personal stance toward religion probably shaped his
overall approach to politics. A traditional Christian's
view of human needs and duties is radically different
from a skeptic's view.

Not surprisingly, scholars disagree over the nature
of Tocqueville's religiosity. Although he was a practicing
Catholic, parts of his correspondence suggest that he
wanted to, but could not affirm the truth of the faith.[1]
This epistolary evidence leads some contemporary
Tocquevillians to conclude that Tocqueville was a skeptic. André Jardin, his most recent biographer, is typical
in this regard. Jardin asserts that Tocqueville became
an unbeliever at age sixteen after reading enlightenment philosophy and that subsequently "Jesus both as
man and God, was apparently absent from his thinking" (Jardin 1988, 62–63).[2]

John C. Lukacs dismisses this evidence, arguing on the basis of different correspondence and Tocqueville's lifelong behavior that he was a sincere Catholic with an "aristocratic, Jansenist, Pascalian bent" (Lukacs 1961, 123n).[3] "Let us be content . . . ," he requests, "that Tocqueville was born a Catholic, that he married in the church, that his English wife became a convert, that he was known and seen attending Mass, that he was cared for by nuns, visited by the parish priest, took the last Sacraments, and was buried in the parish churchyard" (Lukacs 1961, 123).

More recently, Cynthia J. Hinckley has maintained that Tocqueville was at least a devout Christian, if not a believing Catholic. She concludes that the religious distress evidenced in his letters was the "anguish of a believer deprived by the Creator of the unwavering certitude that characterizes faith of the highest order" rather than the "anguish of a skeptic" (Hinckley 1990b, 43, 40). She further contends that Tocqueville's traditional faith was central to his religious–political thought. "Not only did Tocqueville specify Christianity as the hope of liberal democracy," she argues, but "he did so in a manner that took nothing away from Christianity as a revealed religion" (Hinckley 1990b, 49; see also Schleifer 1982, 312–313).

Tocqueville's intellectual affinities provide a good starting point for resolving this dispute. When writing volume two of *Democracy in America,* he "live[d] a bit every day" with three giants of French thought who delved deeply into religious matters (cited in Schleifer 1980, 26; Tocqueville 1950–, 13(1):418). The first was the seventeenth-century Catholic theologian Blaise Pascal (1623–1662) who rationally attempted to prove the necessity of unconditionally surrendering to faith. The latter two, Baron de Montesquieu (1689–1755), and

Jean-Jacques Rousseau (1712–1778), were part of a philosophic tradition which rejected Christianity's metaphysical claims.

Did Tocqueville share Pascal's religious orientation, or was he, along with Montesquieu and Rousseau, a skeptic? Before addressing this question directly, I shall begin by briefly presenting the religious–political principles of his three guides. This account will neither do justice to their subtle and complicated arguments, nor establish direct links between their ideas and Tocqueville's. It will, however, provide a frame of reference which will enable us to better discern Tocqueville's first principles.

PASCAL

Pascal's thought was based on the classic Christian premise that a transcendent reality exists independent of human experience and unknowable by human faculties alone (*Pensées*, 194:65).[4] The Bible, or divine revelation, provides the key to understanding this reality (*Pensées*, 547:173–174). The biblical God is an all-powerful deity who created the world and everything in it. His rule over humanity is wholly just although His justice is not always rationally discernible (*Pensées*, 294:100). This God also acts upon the world in miraculous ways which testify to the truth of His doctrines and strengthen the faith of believers (*Pensées*, 802–805:282–283). For traditional Christians, the greatest of all miracles were the birth and resurrection of Christ who, as mediator and redeemer, restored the harmony between God and humanity severed by Adam's sin.

Pascal, like many great Christian theologians, subscribed to St. Augustine's views on life and government as they appear in the *City of God*.[5] True Christians, Augustine believed, are recipients of God's grace, an undeserved gift which enables them freely to love and exalt Him (Deane 1963, 81–83). The *summum bonum* for these individuals is salvation, a good far surpassing anything attainable in the brief span of mortal existence. Their hope for eternal life leads them to live "after the spirit" or to learn and to obey God's will (*City of God*, 14:1).[6] "The true and only virtue . . . ," Pascal writes, "is to hate self . . . and to seek a truly lovable being to love" (*Pensées*, 485:159). Obeying that "lovable being" requires justice, moderation, charity, chastity, indifference to wealth, and, above all, humility.

Pascal considered true Christians to be part of the perfect Christian community which Augustine called the "City of God." This city consists of all those virtuous recipients of grace destined to enjoy the blessings of heaven (see *Pensées*, 473–483:156–159). It is not to be confused with the visible church which legitimately interprets God's will, but counts the damned as well as the saved among its members (*Pensées* 194:65–66; Deane 1963, 30–31). Nor is it to be confused with the political community whose chief purpose is to maintain external peace and order. Pascal believed the Bible requires Christians to obey the governments of such communities no matter how unjust or incompetent. "True Christians," he remarked, " . . . comply with folly, not because they respect folly, but the command of God, who for the punishment of men has made them subject to these follies" (*Pensées*, 338:114). He sanctioned civil disobedience only when government requires impiety, but prohibited active resistant to political authority under all circumstances (see Beitzinger 1984, 232–233).

Augustine believed that pious rulers should view sovereignty as a "handmaid" of God and use it for the "greatest possible extension of His worship" (*City of God*, 5:24). In pursuing this aim, they can, under certain circumstances, use force to punish heretics and schismatics. The goal of this coercion, Augustine avers, is not to compel dissidents to embrace orthodoxy against their wills, but to make them reconsider their errors and to protect the faithful. Pascal doesn't treat the government's power to enforce orthodoxy in his writings, perhaps because the French government of Louis XIV persecuted his Jansenist allies. Nonetheless, his preference for political absolutism strongly suggests that he agreed with Augustine's overall views on this matter (*Pensées*, 288:103, 312–313:106, 320:108; see Beitzinger 1984, 222–234).[7]

Those individuals who elevate the self above God comprise what Augustine calls the "earthly city" (*City of God*, 14:28). Rejecting the truths of the Bible, they seek to achieve temporal happiness by human means alone (Deane 1963, 30). Most self-oriented people belong to what Pascal calls the "order of the flesh." They have the "body as their object" and seek wealth, power, and carnal pleasure (*Pensées*, 460:152). Those who have "the mind as their object" belong to the "order of the spirit" (*Pensées*, 460). From Pascal's perspective, however, it matters little whether members of the earthly city define happiness materially or spiritually. Even philosophers are damned unless they accept the Bible as the ultimate source of truth (*Pensées*, 430:136, 461, 464:153).

MONTESQUIEU AND ROUSSEAU

In contrast to Pascal, Montesquieu and Rousseau used reason alone to assess the human condition and religion's place in it. Montesquieu's chief complaint against traditional Christianity was that it diminished rather that enhanced the quality of civil life. Sincere Christians, in his view, considered themselves "travelers who should think only of another country," and who should, along the way, sacrifice physical pleasure and temporal well-being for the sake of salvation

(*Persian Letters*, 85:245, 119:308).[8] Their otherworldly orientation depleted the economic and political strength of Christian nations and led to a general decline in Europe's population (*Persian Letters*, 17:305, 116:303–304). See also *The Spirit of the Laws*, 25:4 and 23:4, 21, 26). Christian governments also frequently used biblical teachings—such as submission and obedience to political authority—to maintain oppression. Finally, the Bible's emphasis on orthodoxy fostered a destructive "spirit of proselytism" which, when accompanied by intolerance and zeal, led to mindless disputes, bloody persecutions, and interminable religious warfare (see *The Spirit of the Laws*, 25:13, 14 and *Persian Letters*, 143:353, 161:220, 85:259, 29:174–175).

Despite his aversion to Christianity, Montesquieu thought that free societies require some form of religion to maintain their freedom. People in general are irrational, he believed, and lawlessness and oppression would prevail without religion's moral influence (*The Spirit of the Laws*, 24:2, 8). Montesquieu would have liked to replace Christianity with a civil religion wholly compatible with mild republican government. This religion features a rational, freedom-oriented God, divine punishment for injustice, the sanctity of law, sexual equality, and a new understanding of happiness in which the passions are freed from the negative constraints of the Bible (*Persian Letters*, 116:344–348, 133:256; *The Spirit of the Laws*, 24:2, 8).

Montesquieu realized, however, that instituting such a religion among Christian nations would be immensely difficult and politically dangerous (*The Spirit of the Laws*, 25:11). For this reason, his writings include a set of practical recommendations for reforming Christianity from within. These include emphasizing morality at the expense of doctrine, reinterpreting this morality to suit the needs of a free, commercial republic, and, most important, requiring toleration. This latter policy, he hoped, would eventually force the Christian churches to soften the jealousy which historically divided them (*The Spirit of the Laws*, 24:4, 5, 19, 22, 25:9, 10, 12; *Persian Letters*, 85:258–260; 117:305–306; 46:194).

Although Rousseau's attack against traditional Christianity is more famous and more overt than Montesquieu's, it covers much the same ground. He too criticized the transpolitical and otherworldly faith for being incompatible with free, democratic societies. The terms "Christian republic" are "mutually exclusive," he sarcastically remarked (Rousseau 1978, 130).[9] As he describes it, traditional Christianity fails to promote good citizenship and breeds a general indifference to the public good (Rousseau 1978, 128). "If the state is flourishing," he noted, "[a Christian] barely dares to enjoy the public felicity for fear of becoming proud of his country's glory. If the state declines, he blesses the hand of God that weighs heavily on his people" (Rousseau 1978, 129).

Rousseau also accused Christianity of destroying social unity (Rousseau 1978, 126, 128). Despite its otherworldly orientation, this religion aimed at and succeeded in establishing a "spiritual kingdom" (Rousseau 1978, 126) on earth apart from and superior to civil government. God, the nominal ruler of this "kingdom," required strict obedience, even in cases where the law commanded otherwise. Thus, the clerical interpreters of God's will became the true lawgivers in civil society, determining a citizen's secular obligations and the quality of his citizenship (Rousseau 1978, 127). The clergy also determined the requirements of faith, and by stressing the need for orthodoxy, fostered the theological intolerance which Rousseau, like Montesquieu, abhorred. "It is impossible to live in peace with people whom one believes are damned," Rousseau notes. "To love them would be to hate God who punishes them" (Rousseau 1978, 131).

Finally, and perhaps most important, Rousseau condemned Christians for their tendency both to abuse political power and to suffer political abuse. Christians have a secret desire for dominion, he believed, and will act despotically when given the opportunity (Rousseau 1978, 126). Under a tyrant's boot, however, they become humble and meek, attribute their fate to divine providence, and cling to their heavenly aspirations (Rousseau 1978, 129). Thus, "true Christians are made to be slaves," he laments. "They know it and are scarcely moved thereby; this brief life is of too little worth in their view" (Rousseau 1978, 130).

For these and other reasons, Rousseau also argues that free societies would be better served by a civil religion than by Christianity. His civil religion resembles Montesquieu's in important respects, although it is less friendly to commerce and the physical pleasures and stresses patriotism more than resistance to tyranny. Its positive tenets include "the existence of a powerful, intelligent, beneficent, foresighted, and providential divinity; the afterlife; the happiness of the just; the punishment of the wicked;" and "the sanctity of the social contract and the laws" (Rousseau 1978, 131). These tenets are the "sentiments of sociability" needed for good citizenship rather than theological necessities (Rousseau 1978, 130). Thus, the sovereign will banish a non-believer, "not for being impious, but for being unsociable," that is "for being incapable of sincerely loving the laws, justice, and of giving his life, if need be, for his duty" (Rousseau 1978, 131).

Although Rousseau harshly indicts Christianity, he, like Montesquieu, allows it a role in civil society. There is, in fact, a similarity between the positive dogmas of his civil religion and certain key Christian doctrines. Both feature a monotheistic, providential, benign deity who rewards justice and punishes injustice in the afterlife. More important, Rousseau's citizens may embrace any and all Christian doctrines that are not politically harmful (Rousseau 1978, 131). "The right that the social compact gives the sovereign over the subjects," Rousseau notes, "does not exceed . . . the limits of public utility" (Rousseau 1978, 130). Since Christian theology often adversely affects the interests of civil society, however, the amount of traditional Christianity compatible with a Rousseauan democracy is likely to be small. Staples of Christian orthodoxy such as "*no salvation outside the church*" (Rousseau 1978, 131, his emphasis) would be banished because of their links to intolerance. Such would also be the fate of doctrines which were too otherworldly, which weakened the bonds of citizenship, or which challenged the authority of a legitimate sovereign.

Thus, the differences between the traditional Catholic and the eighteenth-century French philosophical approach to religion and politics are quite clear. For Pascal and Augustine, the Bible is the guide to life—and salvation its ultimate aim. Politics achieves a precarious dignity in their view by establishing peace and otherwise subordinating secular to religious concerns. From a biblical perspective, the very idea of civil religion is blasphemous because its God serves human beings rather than vice versa.

Rousseau and Montesquieu, on the other hand, rejected traditional Christian politics precisely because its theocentric orientation gave short shrift to freedom. Both thinkers recognized, however, that free societies need religion and fashioned civil religions to meet this need. These religions retained certain elements of Christian morality conducive to freedom while dropping others opposed to it, and featured toleration rather than orthodoxy as a central requirement of faith.

TOCQUEVILLE'S FIRST PRINCIPLES

Which perspective on life, the religious or the secular, provided the "common spring" for Tocqueville's thought? I agree with those scholars who consider Tocqueville a skeptic, at least with regard to the truth of divine revelation. While I' think the overall tenor of Tocqueville's correspondence supports this view, I consider his utilitarian approach to religion in the *Democracy* even more conclusive.

Hinckley argues that this approach "is presented in a context that supports, rather than denies, the truthfulness of Christianity" (Hinckley 1990b, 44). There are, in fact, certain passages on religion in the *Democracy* which suggest more than an impersonal, utilitarian analysis. These include references to the purity and ideal quality of the biblical world, praise for a God-oriented conception of virtue, emphatic rejections of materialism, and assertions that a belief in the soul's immortality is "indispensable to man's greatness" (529, 542, 544, 545). These passages testify to Tocqueville's strong admiration for Christianity's spiritual character.

For *Democracy in America* to support the truthfulness of Christianity, however, the book's overall argument would have to be Scripturally based, that is it would have to start from a biblical understanding of human nature and government. It would also have to aim at promoting God-oriented rather than self-oriented behavior. This, at least, is how all traditional Christian thinkers proceeded when writing on politics.

The starting point for Tocqueville's analysis of religion's usefulness is not the Bible, but the human need for metaphysical certainty (433–434). Tocqueville discusses this need exclusively in terms of temporal rather than otherworldly happiness, rarely mentioning service to God as the proper end of faith (433, 434, but see 529). Tocqueville also suggests that reason rather than faith is the best guide to metaphysical truth, and ignorance rather than sin the chief obstacle to attaining it. Rational metaphysical inquiry is a task of unparalleled difficulty, he believed, because of the extraordinary complexity of the questions it addresses (443).

Some sciences, he argues, are both "useful to the crowd" and "within its capacities" (443). This is clearly the case with modern utilitarian ethics and its chief principle, enlightened self-interest (526).[10] Others, like the natural sciences "can be mastered only by the few," but benefit the many who "need nothing beyond their more remote applications" (443, see 459–465). The metaphysical sciences, however, deal with questions which all must resolve, but virtually none can fathom. "Only minds singularly free from the ordinary preoccupations of life, penetrating, subtle, and trained to think," he observed, "can at the cost of much time and trouble sound the depths of these truths that are so necessary" (443).

Religion solves this problem for "the crowd" by answering the "primordial questions" in ways that are "clear, precise, intelligible . . . and very durable" (443). The intellectual surrender it requires is well compensated for by the peace of mind it provides. This is true even for those religions which are "very false and very ridiculous," Tocqueville notes in a functionalist vein (443). "Whether or not they save men's souls in the next world," such religions "greatly contribute to their happiness and dignity in this" (444).

What is appropriate for the crowd, however, is not suitable for the small group of choice minds capable of metaphysical speculation. This group consists of philosophers, not theologians, as Tocqueville's discussion makes clear. Philosophers use the "natural light" of "unaided reason" to explore the mysteries surrounding the first and last things (443). Reason's inability to "sound the depths" of these matters completely, however, inevitably leads to frustration and doubt. For all their efforts, Tocqueville observed, past thinkers have "done no more than discover a small number of contradictory ideas . . . without ever firmly grasping the truth or even finding mistakes that are new" (443). Indeed, in Tocqueville's view, any thinker claiming to know "the supreme good or absolute truth" has more likely abandoned than vindicated his reason (453).

Pascal's awareness of philosophy's limitations led him to embrace Catholicism as Tocqueville knew. Having made this choice, he based his political thought on divine revelation and Church teaching as all Catholic theologians must do, no matter how subtle and penetrating their minds. For these men, the great political question was what political arrangements best served the interests of religion rather than whether religion was politically useful. This concern led Pascal to approve of absolute government for its efficacy in promoting the peace that piety requires. When faced with the same awareness, Tocqueville tried, but could not abandon reason for faith. His rationalism accounts for the lifelong devotion to freedom which distinguishes his philosophical and political careers.[11]

Tocqueville's most concise definition of freedom, or liberty, appears in his "Political and Social Condition of France" published in the *London and Westminster Review* in 1836. This definition clearly illustrates the secular character of his political thought.

> According to the modern, the democratic, and, we venture to say the only just notion of liberty, every man, being presumed to have received from nature the intelligence necessary for his own general guidance, is inherently entitled to be uncontrolled by his fellows in all that only concerns himself, and to regulate at his own will his own destiny.

From the moment when this notion of liberty has penetrated deeply into the minds of the people, and has solidly established itself there, absolute and arbitrary power is thenceforth but a usurpation, or an accident; for, if no one is under any moral obligation to submit to another, it follows that the sovereign will can rightfully emanate only from the union of the wills of the whole. From that time passive obedience loses its character of morality, and there is no longer a medium between the bold and manly virtues of the citizen and the base compliances of the slave (Tocqueville 1836, 166)

Liberty, for traditional Christians, was the realm of freedom which enabled the recipients of God's grace to choose a virtuous life. In the absence of grace, it was inextricably linked to the sinful propensities of life in the earthly city (see Deane 1963, 25–27). Although Tocqueville valued liberty highly as a precondition for virtue, his understanding of the term is largely negative and wholly devoid of religious content (see Lamberti 1989, 53–63 esp. 61). Indeed, this understanding clearly makes the self rather than God the arbiter of its own destiny, even in the realm of religious belief and practice. Further, nature rather than the Bible or any church provides the self with the necessary wherewithal to achieve its goals and randomly distributes its bounty to Christians and non-Christians alike.

Tocqueville's argument for intellectual self-sufficiency here is somewhat disingenuous because, as we have seen, he believed that virtually all people must accept some principle of authority when confronting the ultimate questions. His point, however, is that force is a wholly inappropriate means for establishing this principle which must be consciously or unconsciously chosen by the individual himself.

In this respect, Tocqueville is more like Montesquieu and Rousseau than Pascal. Pascal supported absolute government which he considered all Christians obliged to obey under most circumstances. Tocqueville categorically rejected this idea, asserting with the two philosophers that a "just notion" of liberty requires political freedom and government by consent. These principles, for him, were important components of personal liberty, essential means to its defense, and contrary to the "passive obedience" required by traditional Christianity.

Tocqueville's commitment to democratic freedom was stronger than his commitment to traditional, revealed Christianity—which he was willing to modify when the requirements of the two conflicted. When discussing his recommendations for change, he carefully distinguished between "secondary notions" he felt could be safely dispensed with and the principal opinions of the faith he deemed inviolable (447). As we shall see, however, Tocqueville's proposed modifications of Christianity eliminated more than the unnecessary externals. We shall discuss one such modification here and consider others in the next chapter.

Despite their disagreements on issues large and small, most traditional Christians considered pride a grievous sin and humility a necessary virtue (see, for example, *Pensées*, 493). These valuations were based on biblical passages such as Luke 18:14 which teaches that "everyone who exalts himself should be humbled, and he who humbles himself should be exalted." Pride's chief defect from a Christian point of view is its tendency to elevate worldly above heavenly concerns in people's minds. Indeed, Augustine taught that pride was the primary cause of original sin, and thus the ultimate source of man's alienation from God:

> Whence doth iniquity abound? From pride. Cure pride and there will be no more iniquity. Consequently, that the cause of all diseases might be cured, namely, pride, the Son of God came down and was made low. Why art

thou proud, O man? God, for thee, became low (cited in Deane 1963, 17).

Tocqueville was well aware of the traditional Christian view on these matters as his reference to pride as a vice in the following passage indicates. Nonetheless, he agreed with Montesquieu and Rousseau that this valuation fostered the "base compliances of the slave" rather than the "bold and manly virtues of the citizen."

> Far from thinking that we should council humility to our contemporaries, I wish men would try to give them a higher idea of themselves and of humanity; humility is far from healthy for them; what they most lack, in my view, is pride. I would gladly surrender several of our petty virtues for that one vice (632).

Although Tocqueville's religious functionalism does not in and of itself make him a skeptic, it is noteworthy that in his published writings he never suggests that the Bible is divinely inspired, never disparages the earthly city, and never locates himself within a Christian theological tradition.[12] These omissions tend to confirm that Tocqueville's views on religion as on all else derived from "unaided reason" (443) alone (see Lamberti 1989, 158).

WAS TOCQUEVILLE A RATIONAL CHRISTIAN?

Doris Goldstein agrees that Tocqueville approached religion rationally, but asserts that his ultimate "philosophical position" was "akin to Christianity" (Goldstein 1975, 7). He derived this position through introspection, Goldstein claims, rather than by meditating on Scripture or engaging in abstract metaphysical inquiry (Goldstein 1975, 5–6). Generalizing on the basis of his acquired self-knowledge, Tocqueville arrived at the "psychological realities of human existence" which argued for the truth of core Christian doctrines such as the existence of God, spirituality, and the immortality of the soul (Goldstein 1975, 5–6, 10). For Goldstein's Tocqueville, the "very need for the infinite in human beings" was "proof" for this latter principle's veracity (Goldstein 1975, 6). This view that Christianity is true because it addresses human needs contrasts sharply with the view of Hinckley's Tocqueville that Christianity is true because it is divinely inspired.[13]

Goldstein's conclusion that Tocqueville was a rational or philosophical Christian is based largely on her analysis of his correspondence. In one of his last letters on religious subjects written to Louis-Firmin Bouchitte in 1858, Tocqueville averred that a "small number of very simple ideas, which indeed all men have more or less grasped" led him to:

> belief in a first cause, which remains utterly evident and utterly inconceivable; to the fixed laws which the physical world allows us to see and which we must assume to exist in the moral world; to the Providence of God, hence to His justice; and to the responsibility of man, who has been allowed to know that there is good and evil, hence another life (cited in Lamberti 1989, 156–157; Tocqueville 1860–1866, 7:476).

Tocqueville's personally holding these beliefs would not by itself make him a rational Christian. There are three reasons for this. First, these ideas are not uniquely Christian. In fact, they are as much a part of Montesquieu and Rousseau's civil religion as they are of biblical faith. Second, Tocqueville strongly suggests that "rational Christianity" is a contradiction in terms. "Christianity is not a philosophy but a religion," he once wrote to Gobineau, precisely because it is based so heavily on faith (Tocqueville 1959, 205–206; Tocqueville 1951–, 9:58). Finally, Tocqueville believed, at least in the 1830s, that no metaphysical principles are either simple or understandable by all human beings. In fact, as we have seen, he doubted that even the greatest thinkers could attain certainty regarding such principles, given their infinite complexity and the limitations of time.

If reason and utility were Tocqueville's religious reference points, as Goldstein contends, I should add that it makes little practical difference whether or not he believed certain elements of Christianity to be divinely inspired. Once the self replaces the Bible as the starting point for religious inquiry, orthodoxy becomes malleable, the supernatural suspect, and religion more a human than a divine affair. This shift in starting points also gives Tocqueville license to reshape traditional Christianity according to his own perception of human need. From a traditional Christian perspective Tocqueville was clearly a denizen of the earthly city. At the bar of faith, all philosophers, no matter how great their respect for Christianity, are guilty of pride, a consummate evil in the biblical canon.

Did Tocqueville actually believe in the truth of the previously mentioned ideas? I cannot say. Tocqueville's restless, complex, and subtle mind was constantly preoccupied with the problem of human existence which he considered beyond reason's grasp. In the end, respect for the man cautions against fruitless speculation regarding his final stand on this problem. As his biographer Jardin remarked (although in a slightly different context, "there are intimate reaches of the spirit that compel to silence" (Jardin 1988, 532).[14]

TOCQUEVILLE'S STATURE AS A THINKER

Although most Tocqueville scholars admire him greatly, some demur. Catherine H. Zuckert argues, for example, that Tocqueville wasn't a true philosopher be-

cause he questioned the possibility of acquiring metaphysical knowledge (Zuckert 1991, 121–152). This skepticism, she maintains, caused him to focus on how liberal
democracies actually work rather than on evaluating political alternatives. He fails to "reveal the full range of
political or intellectual possibilities," she asserts, and is
more concerned with "discovering the origins and effects
of what most men think is true" than with "seeking the
truth about human affairs" (Zuckert 1991, 131, 134).

In a similar vein, Thomas G. West accuses Tocqueville
of viewing the political in light of the subpolitical, thereby
downplaying the importance of government and statesmanship and rejecting nature as a standard for justice
and morality (West 1991, 155–177, esp. 158, 175). The
guiding thread behind these criticisms is that Tocqueville
was a "political sociologist" rather than a great political
thinker (see also Anastaplo 1991, 459).

I reject this point of view, joining instead with
those scholars who consider Tocqueville a political
philosopher of the first rank.[15] Leo Strauss defines a
political philosopher as one who attempts to know
"both the nature of political things and the right, or
the good, political order" (Strauss 1959, 12). In pursuing this wisdom, such a person must look beyond
the prevailing opinions of his age toward the realm of
objective truth. Tocqueville was a lifelong seeker after
truth, not flinching when his well-considered views
conflicted with his personal feelings, his class interests, or the spirit of his age (704). All his political
endeavors were guided by moral standards he considered objectively good and just. His critics' failure
to recognize the height of his aspirations if not his
accomplishments, stems in part from their unwilling-
ness to credit his own account of his work. As Wilhelm
Hennis put it, one "bars every possibility of understanding Tocqueville when one is not prepared to

understand him as he himself wanted to be understood" (Hennis 1991, 37).

Tocqueville expressed his political intentions most clearly in the following famous passage from the introduction to the *Democracy*.

> The first duty imposed on those who now direct society is to educate democracy; to put, if possible, new life into its beliefs; to purify its mores; to control its actions; gradually to substitute understanding of statecraft for present inexperience and knowledge of its true interests for blind instincts; to adapt government to the needs of time and place; and to modify it as men and circumstances require. A new political science is needed for a world itself quite new (12).

Tocqueville considered *Democracy in America* a "political–philosophical work" (as he later put it) and viewed himself as a teacher of politics in the grand sense (cited in Schleifer 1980, 83; Tocqueville 1951–1 8(1):176). He set forth a "new political science" in the *Democracy* to enhance the prospects for freedom under the novel conditions brought about by the victory of equality (40). Tocqueville shows in an address delivered to the *Académie des Sciences Morales et Politiques* in 1853 how deeply his concept of "political science" is rooted in a view of human nature. The "scientific" side of politics, he informs us, is

> founded in the very nature of man . . . his interests; his faculties; the needs revealed by philosophy and history; the instincts which change their objects with the times, but never change their nature, and are as immortal as the race itself. It is this aspect [of political science] . . . that teaches us what laws are most appropriate for the general and permanent condition of mankind" (cited in Zetterbaum 1967, 144; Tocqueville 1951–, 16:230).

Tocqueville hoped that his book would influence lawgivers, statesmen, and other groups who "direct society" less formally such as religious figures, artists, and teachers (see Ceasar 1990, 37). Properly educated, these leaders would be equipped to foster prudent and public spirited statesmanship and to encourage needed political reforms. Their primary task, however, would be to strengthen national character by reinvigorating religion, promoting chastity, and shaping private behavior in other politically beneficial ways. This wide-ranging agenda clearly indicates that Tocqueville's sense of the political encompassed the subpolitical rather than being shaped by it.

Zuckert's charge that Tocqueville failed to seek the truth about human affairs also lacks foundation. Tocqueville believed that philosophical statesmanship must operate within the constraints established by the historical era (time and place) of which one is a part. Thus, he thought, as we shall see, that no attempt to maintain freedom could succeed without accepting the triumph of democracy. This did not, however, prevent him from evaluating aristocracy, democracy, and the various forms of government compatible with democracy.

Zuckert's criticism rests, I believe, on the mistaken assumption that the practice of political philosophy requires metaphysical certainty, or an absolute knowledge regarding the soul, the cosmos, and the universe (Zuckert 1991, 131–133, 149–150). This assumption, as Allan Bloom points out, is fatal to all philosophy which properly begins from an awareness of our own ignorance regarding the most important things (Bloom 1990, 20). In my view, Tocqueville shared this Socratic perspective which requires us to build on the wisdom we can acquire while never forgetting what we don't and perhaps can't ever know. Tocqueville did not take pleasure in metaphysical speculation as Socrates did and continually chafed at philosophy's limitations. His anguish, however, was largely due to his inability to escape from the ultimate questions.[16]

CONCLUSION

Tocqueville's rational approach to these questions led him, as we have seen, to judge religion on the basis of its service to freedom, the principle he considered essential for human development and moral choice. Like Montesquieu and Rousseau, Tocqueville argued that religion in some form was necessary to freedom's survival. His political advocacy of religion supports the claim of today's religious functionalists that early liberal thinkers were somewhat more friendly to religion than liberals nowadays suppose. Tocqueville did not believe, however, that traditional Christianity was suitable for free, democratic societies. He therefore sought to replace the biblical faith with a new, more civil religion, Christian in name but secular in orientation. I shall set forth the basic elements of Tocqueville's Christianity in the next chapter.

CHAPTER THREE

TOCQUEVILLE'S CHRISTIANITY

The more people are assimilated to one another and brought to an equality, the more important it becomes that religions, while remaining studiously aloof from the daily turmoil of worldly business, should not needlessly run counter to prevailing ideas or the permanent interests of the mass of the people. For as public opinion becomes ever increasingly the first and most irresistible of powers there is no force outside it to support a prolonged resistance (448).

Tocqueville embellished his description of American religion in *Democracy in America* with a series of recommendations designed to preserve Christianity's power in democratic times (see esp. 447–448). Most scholars treat this descriptive and didactic material together, assuming that Tocqueville simply approved of American faith and wanted French Christianity to emulate it in certain respects (see, for example, Lively 1962, 196, and Hinckley 1990a, 340–341). This is not entirely true. Tocqueville was more critical of American Christianity and more pessimistic about its future than is generally recognized. His guidelines for restructuring

Christianity in the *Democracy* were part of a comprehensive series of recommendations for religious reform
that he hoped would enable France to improve on American arrangements and, by implication, would guide
American religionists in the future. I shall discuss these
recommendations in this chapter.

POETRY AND RELIGION

The starting point for understanding Tocqueville's
"civil" version of Christianity is not his examination of
religion proper, but his treatment of poetry. This treatment, which appears in Bk. II, Pt. I, Chapter 17, of
Democracy in America is entitled, "On Some Sources of
Poetic Inspiration in Democracies" (482–487). Although
this title promises a literary discussion, the chapter
deals with a number of religious themes including the
effects of social condition on the character of religion,
democratic and aristocratic conceptions of God and
providence, and the aspects of human nature which
make religion necessary.[1]

Tocqueville suggests that poetry arises from the pa-
thos of the human condition which he describes in
Pascalian terms: "man comes from nothing, passes
through time, and disappears forever in the bosom of
God. He is seen but for a moment wandering on the
verge of two abysses, and then is lost" (487). Without
some understanding of this moment, we would be incapable of poetry because "one cannot describe what
one does not conceive." Comprehending it fully, however, we would also lack poetry because imagination would
have no important field for action. But, "the nature of
man is sufficiently revealed for him to know something of
himself and sufficiently veiled to leave much in impen-
etrable darkness, a darkness in which he ever gropes,
forever in vain, trying to understand himself" (487).

Through the use of imagination, the religious poet makes this reality tolerable by creating a moral and intellectual frame of reference which enables human beings to function without being crippled by existential doubt. This frame of reference constitutes the essence of religion for Tocqueville, as we have seen. Its creation requires a certain manipulation of the truth, a certain forced ennobling of nature, but this distortion is on the whole salubrious and wise. It is "not the poet's function to portray reality," he remarks, "but to beautify it and offer the mind some loftier image" (483; see Lawler 1991, 106–108).

To properly accomplish this task, the religious poet must search for and represent the ideal (483). In devising an ideal response to life's primordial questions, he must be sensitive to the "activities, feelings, and ideas" of his audience and, most especially, to the state of its imaginative faculties (483). The faculties are shaped to a large extent by the prevailing social condition which ultimately determines the type of religion a people will accept. This accounts for the decidedly different character of popular religion in aristocratic and democratic times (483, 486).

The key distinguishing mark of an aristocratic society is an inequality of conditions accepted by all classes as natural and eternal. This state of affairs fosters a high degree of social stability which disposes the mind to embrace "positive" religions which support the status quo (483). Social inequality also connects people by a network of obligations which inclines them, at least in theory, toward altruism. Aristocratic poets should build on these tendencies, Tocqueville advises, emphasizing belief and fashioning the moral precepts of their religions around self-forgetting behavior (483). This was done in aristocratic Europe where Christian orthodoxy reigned and the "official doctrine of morality" was to "do good without self-interest, as God himself does" (525).

Inequality also shapes the form and scope of religion congenial to aristocracies. Though open to monotheism, these societies generally put "intermediate powers between God and man," support hierarchical ecclesiastical structures, and cherish the symbols and external ceremonies which concretize belief (483). Accustomed to respect traditional authority, aristocratic peoples also tolerate religion regulating virtually every aspect of their lives. Finally, such religion enhances its credibility by glorifying the past. Ancient accounts of heroic deeds assisted by God, for example, will strongly impress aristocratic peoples. Such deeds always "seem grander and more mysterious as they recede into the distance," Tocqueville laconically notes (484).

DEMOCRATIC RELIGION

Tocqueville sets forth detailed guidelines for fashioning democratic religion in the *Democracy*, perhaps to provide guidance for would-be religious poets.[2] People are inclined to adopt very general, vast, and simple religious ideas as democracy spreads, he contends (486). Modern theologians, therefore, should portray God as a "unique and all-powerful Being who dispense[s] the same laws equally and in the same way to all men" (446–447). They should also avoid encumbering their faith with secondary powers such as demons and angels and should under no circumstances give these corporeal form or a direct role in human affairs (486).

Modern theologians must also portray divine providence in a "newer and brighter light" than their traditional counterparts (486). Democrats tend to be skeptical, future- rather than past-oriented, and more concerned than aristocrats with the fate of humanity as a whole. While accounts of supernatural phenomena are likely to leave them cold, they thrill to the ideas of temporal progress, the conquest of nature, and the indefinite perfectibility of the human race (485–486). Writers who connect these ideas to God's designs, Tocqueville notes, will be "admired and understood, for the imagination of their contemporaries is following the same road" (486).

Because democrats who distrust traditional authority adopt dogmatic opinions reluctantly, democratic religion should restrict its sovereignty solely to religious matters and resist the inclination to theologize about politics, law, and science (445). They should also pay no more attention to external ceremonies, forms, and symbols than is absolutely necessary to "fix the human spirit in the contemplation of abstract truths" (447). The most important of these truths by far is the existence of the soul. "Belief in an immaterial and immortal principle, for a time united to matter," is "indispensable to man's greatness," Tocqueville notes (544).

Finally, democratic religion should emphasize moral behavior over doctrinal orthodoxy, which has little appeal to the skeptical democratic mind. This emphasis will strengthen religion while serving the causes of tolerance and civic peace. To be effective, however, religious morality must accommodate itself to the passion for self-interest, the "only stable point in the human heart" (239).[3] In practice, this passion translates into an all-encompassing desire for material well-being. While religion can "purify, control, and restrain" this desire, opposing it completely would jeopardize its survival (448).

Tocqueville's final recommendation is that democratic religion defer to the majority in all cases where this can be done without compromising its integrity.

> The more people are assimilated to one another and brought to an equality, the more important it becomes that religions, while remaining studiously aloof from the daily turmoil of worldly business, should not needlessly run counter to prevailing ideas or the permanent inter-

ests of the mass of the people. For as public opinion becomes ever increasingly the first and more irresistible of powers there is no force outside it to support a prolonged resistance (448).

Part of Tocqueville's religious statesmanship was to play the role of democratic poet, and in so doing to make Western Christianity more serviceable to freedom. At first glance, Tocqueville seems to suggest that all religions when properly reformed are politically valuable, and therefore fit subjects for his artistry. The following passage from *Democracy* illustrates this seeming impartiality:

> Every religion places the object of man's desires outside and beyond worldly goods and naturally lifts the soul into regions far above the realm of the senses. Every religion also imposes on each man some obligations toward mankind, to be performed in common with the rest of mankind, and so draws him away, from time to time, from thinking about himself. That is true even of the most false and dangerous religions (444, 445)

Jack Lively and Marvin Zetterbaum conclude from such statements that Tocqueville considered all religions basically similar "from the point of view of social discipline and morality" (Lively 1962, 184; see also Zetterbaum 1967, 116).[4] Although Tocqueville did see some political value in all spiritually-oriented religions, he subtly shows that only a democratic version of Christianity could promote freedom effectively.

His first step in establishing the legitimacy of his civil religion is to define religion's purpose in a highly restrictive way. "The chief aim of a religion," he writes in the *The Old Regime and the Revolution,*

> is to regulate both the relations of the individual man with his Maker and his rights and duties towards his fellow men on a universal plane, independently, that is

to say, of the views and habits of the social group of which he is a member. The rules of conduct thus enjoined apply less to the man of any given nation or period than to man in his capacity of son, father, master, servant, neighbor (Tocqueville 1955, 11).

Tocqueville's understanding of religion has a clearly modern, democratic cast which virtually excludes all non-Christian faiths. This is evident from the strong emphasis Tocqueville places on the universalistic aspects of religion, that is, the concern of religion for all human beings equally, apart from their political relationships. Neither of the two forms of ancient religion, traditional Judaism or classical paganism were concerned with rights and duties on a universal plane or with the "man-in-himself," independent of his social group (Tocqueville 1955, 11). Although traditional Judaism contained elements of universality, its racial distinctions and different sets of rights and duties for Jews and Gentiles made it a tribal religion in Tocqueville's view (Tocqueville 1955, 12; Tocqueville 1959, 191, 305).[5]

The pagan religions were "always more or less linked up with the political institutions and the social order of their environment, and their dogmas were conditioned to some extent by the interests of the nations, or even the cities, where they flourished" (Tocqueville 1955, 12). Thus, their primary concern was not for all human beings equally, apart from their political relationships, but rather to promote patriotism and good citizenship. This concern necessarily gave them a parochial perspective.

Finally, Islam, the chief contemporary religious rival of Christianity, was also defective according to modern standards because the Koran contained "political maxims, criminal and civil laws, and scientific theories" as well as religious doctrines (445).[6] "That alone," he concluded, "among a thousand reasons, is enough to show that Islam will not be able to hold its power long in ages of enlightenment and democracy, while Christianity is destined to reign in such ages as in all others" (445).[7]

Although Tocqueville speaks optimistically here about Christianity's democratic prospects, he was not sanguine about the survival of traditional Catholicism or Protestantism. Traditional Catholicism, as Tocqueville described it, was more closely linked to Europe's aristocratic class structure than befits a genuine religion. The church's hierarchical makeup, its tendency to support aristocratic, and even absolute governments, and its reliance on secondary agents to propitiate God reflected this linkage (446; see 94). While traditional Protestants were somewhat more democratic than traditional Catholics, they leaned too heavily on the Old Testament's vision of history and its barbarous legal code to retain democratic adherents (36–37, 41–43). Finally, while both these faiths supported morality in ways he considered valuable, their excessive otherworldliness, their reliance on miracles and prophesy, their extensive intrusions into secular life, and their preoccupation with obscure theological questions rendered them unfit for Tocqueville's purposes.

Tocqueville feared that equality would bring traditional Catholicism and Protestantism "crashing down" or simplify them beyond recognition and usefulness (483). Lively and Zetterbaum conclude that to forestall this danger, Tocqueville sought to replace these faiths with relatively contentless spiritual or social "myths" (Zetterbaum 1967, 122–123; Lively 1962, 197). Both scholars criticize Tocqueville for this move on the grounds that it was likely to increase rather than decrease skepticism. "Propagating such salutary myths," Zetterbaum asserts, "cannot but weaken genuine religious belief rather than strengthening it, for by propagating them men are emboldened to consider religion from a functional point of view" (Zetterbaum 1967, 122).

Although Tocqueville was in fact willing to sacrifice genuine religion to meet the needs of democratic society, his religious statesmanship was far more daring and complex than Lively and Zetterbaum suggest. While aware of the shortcomings of traditional Christianity from a democratic perspective, he thought that any attempt to establish a "new religion" in modern times would be "ridiculous and unreasonable." Democratic peoples "will not easily believe in divine missions," he warned, and "will be quick to laugh at new prophets" (435).

A NEW CHRISTIANITY

Tocqueville's solution to this dilemma, I think, was to fashion a democratic version of Christianity which retained only those elements of the traditional faiths compatible with freedom. Tocqueville does not present his version of Christianity systematically, but rather in scattered references throughout his writings and correspondence. Nor does he dot all its i's or cross all its t's. In proceeding cautiously like this, he hoped to blur the differences between his religion and the traditional Christian faiths. By silently eliminating illiberal doctrines or replacing them with democratic counterparts, he would gradually put "new life" into society's beliefs without upsetting its settled convictions (12).

Tocqueville equates his version of Christianity with Gospel Christianity apart from the "historical vehicles in which it was often forced to travel" (Tocqueville 1959, 205). Although its relation to the Gospels is somewhat ambiguous, Tocqueville's Christianity fits comfortably within his own criteria for democratic faith and within the parameters of Montesquieu and Rousseau's civil religions. Its deity is "one sole God, creator and pre-server of all things" rather than the complicated triune deity of traditional Christian theology (446). Tocqueville rarely, as we have seen, refers to Christ as divine or mentions other supernatural phenomena associated with the traditional faith. He also deemphasizes traditional Christianity's distinction between the saved and the damned while stressing its universalistic, egalitarian aspects (Tocqueville 1959, 305).

Tocqueville's portrayal of divine providence is also consistent with democratic sensibilities. According to his account, God prepared humanity for Christ's com-ing by uniting "a great part of mankind, like an im-mense flock, under the scepter of the Caesars" (446). The equal vulnerability, insignificance, and legal status of the diverse peoples under Rome's aegis disposed them to accept the Christian concept of equal rights and duties without cavil (446). Christianity's auspicious be-ginning marked the start of the irreversible democratic revolution which Tocqueville credits with transforming the West. He describes the providential character of this revolution in the following way:

> Everywhere the diverse happenings in the lives of peoples have turned to democracy's profit; all men's efforts have aided it, both those who intended this and those who had no such intention, those who fought for democracy and those who were the declared enemies thereof; all have been driven pell-mell along the same road, and all have worked together, some against their will and some unconsciously, blind instruments in the hands of God.

> Therefore the gradual progress of equality is something fated. The main features of this progress are the follow-ing: it is universal and permanent, it is daily passing beyond human control, and every event and every man helps it along (11–12).[8]

Tocqueville's account of human beings as "blind instruments in the hands of God" does not sit well with his abhorrence of deterministic theories which deny the existence of human freedom (544–545). In fact, as we shall see in the next chapter, he specifically criticizes democratic historians for promoting passivity by portraying people as wholly dependent on circumstances beyond their control (496). Tocqueville resolves this dilemma by staking out a political realm free from necessity. Although his God has drawn a "predestined circle" around his contemporaries which precludes a return to aristocracy, He has made them wholly responsible for determining "whether equality is to lead to servitude or freedom, knowledge or barbarism, prosperity or wretchedness" (705).

A brief comparison of Tocqueville's view of divine providence with St. Augustine's view of the matter will disclose its novelty. According to Augustine, God's purpose in directing human history is to bring about the world's end, the Last Judgment, and eternal peace and happiness for the small, saved portion of the human race. It is most emphatically not to establish democracy or to cause a generalized improvement in temporal well-being. While Augustine's human beings, like Tocqueville's, determine a portion of their own destiny, their choice of good over evil ultimately depends less on themselves than on God's unmerited gift of grace. Finally, Augustine's understanding of providence is based entirely on divine revelation. Tocqueville suggests that God's workings in history are rationally explicable. "God does not Himself need to speak for us to find sure signs of His will;" he concludes. "It is enough to observe the customary progress of nature and the continuous tendency of events" (12; Deane 1963, 71–74).

Tocqueville subtly downplays the significance of dogma in his presentation of Christianity, although he considered some dogma essential to religion. After criticizing Islam (and by implication Judaism) for its overinvolvement with science, law, and politics, he asserts that the Gospels "deal only with the general relations between man and God and between man and man" (445). "Beyond that," he continues, "they teach nothing and do not oblige people to believe anything" (445). Tocqueville says very little about the "chief opinions" of the Gospel essential to his version of Christianity (447). At most, they include a belief in divine providence, the existence of the soul and the afterlife, and divine reward and punishment. These doctrines, while common to all versions of Christianity, are also remarkably close to the main principles of Montesquieu and Rousseau's civil religions.

Traditional Christian theology was as much concerned with the mysteries surrounding God's complex nature as with the "general relations" described above. Indeed, it was controversies over these and other cosmological mysteries which divided and often bloodied the Christian world as anyone well knows who has read Pascal, Augustine, and other traditional Christian theologians. By excluding these subjects from the scope of necessary Christian belief, Tocqueville dramatically expands the traditional definitions of who is a Christian and strikes a blow for theological toleration. Although Tocqueville preferred the intolerance inevitably connected with prescribed belief to a total absence of dogma, he defanged this intolerance by insisting on the separation between church and state (Tocqueville 1959, 206).

Tocqueville's clearest statement on the moral content of his version of Christianity appears in some early correspondence with Artur de Gobineau, his friend and protégé.[9] Here Tocqueville asserts that Christianity accomplished three dramatic changes in the ethical understanding of the West. The first was to elevate the "milder virtues" such as "neighborly love, pity," and "the forgetfulness even of injuries" above the "rude and half-savage virtues" of the ancients. The second was to broaden the realm of duties from "certain citizenries" to humanity as a whole placing in "grand evidence the equality, the unity, the fraternity of all men." The third was to put the "ultimate aim of human life beyond this world," thus giving morality a "finer, purer, less material, less interested, and higher character" (Tocqueville 1959, 191; Tocqueville 1951–, 9:45–46).

Although Tocqueville accepts much of traditional Christian morality as we can see here, he changes it in subtle ways to make it more compatible with democratic principles. First, he downplays or omits certain Christian virtues such as humility which he considered harmful to democrats. Second, he transforms the traditional Christian indifference to government to support for liberal democracy. Tocqueville believed there is a natural tendency for people to harmonize their political opinions with their religious beliefs. "The spirit of man, left to follow its bent," he remarked, "will regulate political society and the City of God in uniform fashion" (287). Building on this tendency, Tocqueville developed the Christian doctrine of equal freedom, which traditionally concerned salvation alone, into the moral basis for government by consent. His version of Christianity does not countenance submission to tyranny.

Finally, he deemphasized the otherworldly, altruistic character of Christian morality by grounding it firmly in the doctrine of self-interest. Tocqueville's correspondence with Gobineau confirms his intention. Shortly after Tocqueville completed Volume II of the *Democracy*, he embarked on a project with Gobineau to determine precisely what was new in the doctrines of the moral philosophers who wrote in the period preceding the French Revolution (Tocqueville 1959, 190; Tocqueville 1951–, 9:45). Gobineau held the view, popular among certain scholars today, that these thinkers initiated a radical break with Christianity by setting forth, among other things, a secular theory of rights and a scheme of public and private morality devoid of religious content (Tocqueville 1959, 195–204; Tocqueville 1951–, 9:49–56).

Tocqueville sharply disagreed with Gobineau, arguing that both the new concept of rights and the new ethical system were derived from Christian principles. Christianity, as he portrays it, was the first system of thought to "put in grand evidence" the idea that everyone has an equal right to worldly goods. Building on this principle, modern moralists taught that "*all* men have a right to certain goods, to certain pleasures, and that our primary moral duty is to procure these for them." This concept of social welfare, which basically extended the principle of equality itself "has now," Tocqueville approvingly remarked, "gained immense breadth, and . . . appears in an endless variety of aspects" (Tocqueville 1959, 193; Tocqueville 1951–, 9:47, emphasis in the text).

Tocqueville also suggests that the concept of enlightened self-interest has a Christian foundation. Modern moralists did not design utilitarian ethics to break with Christianity, he argued, but rather to preserve the essence of Christian morality from the democratic skepticism that was undermining the traditional, otherworldly faith. Their greatest concern was to establish the Christian idea of human brotherhood and its attendant virtues on a secure basis. Thus, they provided secular rewards for these virtues while tailoring them to meet the new and now legitimate concern with material needs and pleasures (Tocqueville 1959, 192–193, 206–208, 211; Tocqueville 1951–, 9:46, 58–60, 67–68).

CONCLUSION

By now it should be clear that French political philosophy is a more plausible source for Tocqueville's religious–political thought than Christian theology. Tocqueville judged religion, as did Montesquieu and Rousseau, by its service to freedom rather than to God. This secular orientation clearly distinguished his approach from that of Pascal, Augustine, and all other traditional Christian theologians. Tocqueville also agreed with these philosophers that traditional Christianity was too enmeshed in Western mores to be replaced, although it ill-served freedom in some respects. Thus he followed their lead in structuring his civil religion around certain politically efficacious Christian doctrines while modifying or eliminating those he considered harmful.

Montesquieu and Rousseau's civil religions differed considerably from each other, although both aimed at preserving freedom. While Montesquieu designed his creed to promote good citizenship, its main function was to protect the private realm from undue government interference. Thus, it limited political power and, as Thomas L. Pangle put it, "was not in conflict with comfort and commerce" (Pangle 1973, 257). Rousseau's civil religion, in contrast, emphasized service to the state and subordinated personal freedom to political freedom as embodied in the general will. These traits gave it a spartan quality which made it hostile to the private pursuit of pleasure or wealth.

John C. Koritansky considers Rousseau the true godfather of Tocqueville's civil religion (Kortansky 1990, 389–400; see also Zetterbaum 1967, 110). In his view, Tocqueville like Rousseau defined freedom as "obedience to self-made law" and required "the full subjection of the individual to the social contract" (Koritansky 1990, 391, 392).

Koritansky's Tocqueville also linked his civil religion to Rousseau's concept of perfectibility which became, in an American context, the "indefinite perfectibility" of man (Koritansky 1990, 396–397). This principle provided the religious dimension for enlightened self-interest, America's "mode of articulation for the general will" (Koritansky 1990, 395, 396). The "official" religion which complemented these doctrines, Koritansky contends, was a contentless version of Protestantism whose only principle was sincerity or an "honest conscience" (Koritansky 1990, 398–399).

Koritansky correctly asserts, as we shall see, that in Tocqueville's eyes America's core beliefs in the 1830s were secular. He somewhat overstresses the humanistic elements of Tocqueville's civil religion, though, while shortchanging its Christian and theistic elements. Although Tocqueville's Christianity does deemphasize orthodoxy in favor of sincerity of belief, it is not as contentless as Koritansky suggests. Indeed, its dogmas are strikingly similar to the positive tenets of Rousseau's civil religion, a fact Koritansky fails to notice.

Koritansky's most grievous error, however, is to assert that Tocqueville's idea of freedom was "essentially Rousseauean" (Koritansky 1990, 391). Tocqueville advocated participatory democracy as Rousseau did, but more as a means to securing individual freedom than as an end in itself. Tocqueville believed, in contrast to Rousseau, that man "is inherently entitled to be uncontrolled by his fellows in all that only concerns himself" (Tocqueville 1836, 166). He therefore never countenanced the surrender of rights to an all-powerful government no matter how democratic.

I believe that Montesquieu had a greater influence than Rousseau on Tocqueville's religious–political ideas.[10] Tocqueville, following Montesquieu, designed his civil religion primarily to protect the private rights of individuals. His difference from Rousseau in this regard becomes especially clear, as we shall see, in his discussion of the tyranny of the majority and other democratic threats to freedom (Lamberti 1989, 62). Tocqueville's civil religion, like Montesquieu's was also more hospitable to acquisitiveness and commercial hustle-bustle than Rousseau thought wise. Only in family matters does Tocqueville's civil religion have a distinctly Rousseauean cast. While Montesquieu's God favors a loosening of sexual mores and the claims of women to full sexual equality, Tocqueville following Rousseau uses religion to support chastity and a modified form of patriarchy.[11]

Although Tocqueville's civil religion was built on a framework designed by others, we must not lose sight of its originality. Tocqueville was the first great political philosopher to reform Christianity in the light of modern democratic conditions. He also treats Christianity more favorably than either Montesquieu or Rousseau. In contrast to these men whose hatred for the religion was barely disguised, Tocqueville genuinely admired Christianity and considered it, on the whole, a positive force in Western history. Tocqueville's religious reforms aimed at insuring that Christianity would survive and provide democratic freedom with crucial political support. Implementing these reforms, he thought, was a task for statesmanship of the highest order.

CHAPTER FOUR

TOCQUEVILLE'S RELIGIOUS STATESMANSHIP

The importance of mores is a universal truth to which study and experience continually bring us back. I find it occupies the central position in my thoughts; all my ideas come back to it in the end (308).

Tocqueville wrote at a time in European history when serious thinkers questioned the very possibility of statesmanship. Hegel, German socialists, French positivists, and racialists were arguing with varying degrees of popular success that history's political actors were little more than ciphers, the pawns of forces beyond their control (Lively 1962, 34–35). Tocqueville devoted considerable energy to refuting these views which he hated. In fact, he based his hopes for religious reform on the proposition that statesmanship mattered. But what could statesmen actually accomplish in history, and what interests did religious and liberal statesmen have in common? I shall examine Tocqueville's answers to these questions in this chapter.

I shall also briefly consider Tocqueville's analysis of French religious–political history in the late eighteenth and early nineteenth centuries. Tocqueville thought an

61

understanding of France's failure to manage church–state affairs well during this period was essential to understanding America's successful use of religion to maintain freedom. When considered together, his accounts of French and American religious statesmanship provide powerful object lessons on how statecraft can enhance or diminish a country's political health.

THE SCOPE OF STATESMANSHIP

Tocqueville's most comprehensive treatment of the scope of statesmanship in *Democracy in America* occurs in the chapter entitled "Some Characteristics Peculiar to Historians in Democratic Centuries" (493–496). Here Tocqueville describes and evaluates the way aristocratic and democratic historians view the role of statesmen and other great individuals in human affairs. Aristocratic historians, as he portrays them, focus on the "few leading actors" of a particular era who capture the public eye (494). They attribute historical events to the "will and character" of these individuals and seek to discern the "secret motives" that make them tick. They also give chance a considerable role in human affairs (493, 494). Democratic historians, on the other hand, are systematizers. They attribute little influence to extraordinary individuals, seeking instead to understand the "great general causes" that work beneath the surface of things. They hold these causes responsible for even the "smallest particular events" (493–494).

Tocqueville does not simply endorse nor dismiss either view of history. He praises aristocratic historians for giving certain great individuals their due, but criticizes them for shortchanging general causes and failing to perceive the interconnectedness of things. They tend to ignore, for example, the web of social factors which lift certain individuals onto the stage of history while consigning others, no less worthy, to oblivion. On the other hand, he faults democratic historians for over-systematizing and reducing men and societies to unconscious pawns in the grip of some "superior dominating force" (495). He feared that if the democratic approach to history prevailed, a fatalistic view of life would paralyze society, undermine human dignity, and inevitably lead to tyranny (494–496).

Tocqueville's own method of historical analysis was to draw on the measure of truth in both views, varying the proportion he used according to the particular historical epoch he was studying. He suggests that historians analyzing aristocracies are right to concentrate on particular influences because the masses in those societies were malleable and powerless. In modern democracies, however, individuals rarely achieve great distinction. Thus democratic historians are right to focus on the complex set of interrelated factors that reveal the overall character of a society.[1] Although not a determinist, Tocqueville predicted the future with astonishing accuracy in some cases because of his ability to understand these factors.[2]

The following passage in *Democracy in America*, where statesmen appear like somewhat helpless navigators, suggests that Tocqueville favors the democratic view of history:

> Sometimes, after a thousand efforts, a lawgiver succeeds in exercising some indirect influence over the destiny of nations, and then his genius is praised, whereas it is often the geographical position of the country, over which he has no influence, a social state which has been created without his aid, mores and ideas whose origin he does not know, and a point of departure of which he is unaware that give to society impetuses of irresistible force against which he struggles in vain and which sweep him, too, along.

> A lawgiver is like a man steering his route over the sea. He, too, can control the ship that bears him, but he cannot change its structure, create winds, or prevent the ocean stirring beneath him (163).

In this passage, Tocqueville enumerates a variety of constraints on democratic statesmanship including the geography of a country, the nature of its founding, and its social state. These factors seem to narrow the realm of political choice, making it possible for lawgivers to exert only indirect influence at best and this only with Herculean effort. On closer examination, though, we find that his prognosis for democratic statesmanship is not as bleak as it first appears. Democratic statesmen do matter, but their influence is "better hidden, more complex, less powerful, and hence less easy to sort out and trace" than that of their aristocratic counterparts (494).

In contrast to many European historians and philosophers, Tocqueville generally downplayed the role of geography and climate in human affairs. "Physical causes do not influence the destiny of nations as much as is supposed," he asserted (306). Of course, Tocqueville readily conceded that geography was unusually kind to America. The country's splendid isolation from Europe and its seemingly inexhaustible natural resources contributed to its unique political health and economic prosperity. Yet while Latin America enjoyed similar advantages, its nations were warlike, impoverished, and underpopulated. In the last analysis, similar geographical circumstances do not necessarily produce analogous political results (306).

Tocqueville also discounted the significance of geography on sexual morality, a subject which he considered of great political significance. Although he admitted that climate affects the intensity of eros, he thought weather less relevant to a country's sexual mores than its religious, social, and political institutions (590, 594–595). History teaches that a nation of constant climate can experience sharp changes in its sexual life as a result of regime changes. Such was the case in France after the Revolution. In the last years of the Old Regime, license was prevalent among a corrupt aristocracy while the vast majority of Frenchmen were chaste by habit and conviction. Although the upheaval caused by the Revolution unsettled the sexual morals of the masses, it returned the remnants of the old aristocracy to their once respectable moral standards (599–600).

Tocqueville felt that statesmen are significantly hampered by ignorance of their country's origins, an ignorance which limits their insight into the complexity and seeming irrationality of its political affairs. In Europe where national beginnings are "concealed in the darkness of the past," this barrier to an adequate knowledge of politics is insurmountable. No such barrier exists in America, however. America's founders left voluminous records of their doings which illuminated their country's "point of departure" with unprecedented clarity. Tocqueville's analysis of America was, by his own admission, greatly enhanced by his ability to study America's origins comprehensively (32).

Tocqueville did believe, as we have seen, that one constraint on statesmanship was highly significant and universally operative: the social state or social condition. This he roughly defined as the dominant principle governing human relationships in a particular society. He describes the importance of the social state as an explanatory factor in politics in the following famous passage from the *Democracy:*

> The social state is commonly the result of circumstances, sometimes of laws, but most often of a combi-

nation of the two. But once it has come into being, it may
itself be considered as the prime cause of most of the
laws, customs, and ideas which control the nation's
behavior; it modifies even those things which it does not
cause (50).

Tocqueville argued that two social states shaped
the course of Western history: inequality and equality,
the touchstones of aristocracy and democracy respectively. He begins *Democracy in America* by tracing the
rise of democracy at the expense of aristocracy, a growth
which he attributes at some points to divine providence
and at other points to a complex set of human factors.
Tocqueville thought that, whatever its cause, the gradual
progress of equality was something inevitable (9–12).[3]

Throughout his work, Tocqueville strongly advises
his contemporaries to recognize democracy as the basic
fact of modern political life. No lawgiver "however wise
or powerful," he asserts, could function effectively "without making equality his first principle and watchword"
(695). This was true both in the United States where
political life was conceived in equality and in France
where revolution established equality without fully destroying the vestiges of the Old Regime.

Some scholars, as we saw in chapter 2, argue on
the basis of assertions like this that Tocqueville considered politics a kind of epiphenomenon, a mere byproduct
or reflection of deeper realities. If Tocqueville viewed
politics in this way, he did indeed leave little room for
statesmanship. As Marvin Zetterbaum put it, "Thinking
of political entities in terms of social condition does not
make the concept of political life meaningless, but it
considerably diminishes the importance of political life
as a social force" (Zetterbaum 1967, 138).

Tocqueville argued strongly, however, that while
democracy does circumscribe statesmanship considerably, statesmen *could* determine the critical issue of

modern political life: whether equality would lead to slavery or freedom (705). In so doing, Tocqueville gave his democratic view of history a sharply aristocratic twist. He did not assert that democratic statesmen can affect the course of political life as powerfully or straightforwardly as their aristocratic counterparts (494). Nonetheless, they can, he believed, play a decisive role in preserving what Tocqueville considered the greatest political good.

MORES

How can such statesmen most effectively serve the cause of freedom? Most American political writers, like the authors of *The Federalist Papers*, thought that the chief task of statesmanship is to design laws and institutions which directly prevent the abuse of power.[4] Tocqueville disagreed. He admired the American laws and institutions designed for this purpose (although not uncritically) and devoted considerable attention to them in his work. Yet he points out that their excellence stemmed from their compatibility with the "genius" of the American people and were not simply transferable to alien political terrain (307).

Mexican statesmen learned this lesson the hard way. Wishing to establish a federal system, they took the American Constitution as a model and copied it almost completely. But "when they borrowed the letter of the law," Tocqueville notes, "they could not at the same time transfer the spirit that gave it life" (165). As a sad result, Mexico during Tocqueville's time was "constantly shifting from anarchy to military despotism and back from military despotism to anarchy" (165).

Tocqueville thought that character was more vital than laws and institutions to the maintenance of freedom. In this respect, he followed Rousseau who argued in *The Social Contract* that mores rather than laws form the "unshakable keystone" of a free society (Rousseau 1978, 77). Rousseau believed that good character binds a people together and makes them willing to accept the responsibilities of citizenship. Tocqueville agreed. "How could society escape destruction," he asked, "if, when political ties are relaxed, moral ties are not tightened" (294)? Healthy mores can preserve a country's freedom in the absence of good laws, he observed, but no laws can save a country whose character is degraded.

Tocqueville defined character or mores as the "sum of the moral and intellectual dispositions of men in society" (305n8).[5] These include a people's oddities of behavior as well as their politically significant habits and beliefs (32, 48). Tocqueville's stress on the statesman's responsibility for promoting good mores was the distinctive feature of his politics, setting the agenda for his "new political science" and his rhetorical strategy in the *Democracy* (12). James W. Ceaser has called this aspect of a statesman's work "superintendence," a term I shall occasionally use when discussing Tocqueville's views on character building (Caesar 1990, 20). Although Tocqueville doesn't use the term, it perfectly captures his sense of this difficult and multifaceted task.

Tocqueville believed that successful superintendence requires a thorough understanding of democratic public opinion. Thus, he analyzes equality's effects on mores at great length in the *Democracy*, paying special attention to democracy's distinctive moral and intellectual horizon. His major goal, of course, was to teach statesmen which democratic character traits maintain and which subvert freedom. "The essence of the lawgiver's art," Tocqueville notes, "is by anticipation to appreciate these natural bents of human societies in order to know where the citizens' efforts need support and where there is more need to hold them back" (543).

Successful superintendence also requires a knowledge of democracy's political resources. Although Tocqueville believed, as we shall see, that a variety of democratic principles and practices were conducive to good character, he thought, at least in the 1830s, that Christianity topped the list. "Despotism may be able to do without faith," he wrote in a famous passage of the *Democracy*, "but freedom cannot" (294). Thus, "lawgivers" and "all upright educated men" who wish to secure freedom must "raise up the souls of their fellow citizens and turn their attention toward heaven" (543).

Finally, democratic statesmen must learn to apply their acquired wisdom to the unique circumstances of their own place and time. A successful strategy for strengthening character in Tocqueville's America may not work in Tocqueville's France or in America of the 1990s. Making such judgments requires flexibility, imagination, and intuition—skills which can't easily be taught. Ultimately, there is no set formula for promoting religion, good character, or freedom. As Tocqueville put it: "different times make different demands. The goal alone is fixed to which humanity should press forward; the means of getting there ever change" (543).

CHRISTIANITY AND ENLIGHTENMENT

The lawgivers and upright educated men Tocqueville had in mind when arguing for religion's usefulness were probably French liberal democrats hostile to Christianity. Tocqueville also frequently reminded French traditionalists that equality and freedom were not responsible for their Church's sorry state. His rhetorical goal in making these points was to promote respect, if not friendship, between long-time adversaries who, in his judgment, bore considerable responsibility for France's future well being (16–18).

Tocqueville's case for reconciliation between the two groups was based on a careful study of the roots of their enmity. He begins by linking their schism to some "accidental and particular cause" rather than to a natural antipathy (300). "The notion that democratic regimes are necessarily hostile to religion," he wrote, "is based on a total misconception of the facts; nothing in the Christian faith or even in Roman Catholicism is incompatible with democracy and, on the contrary, it would seem that a democratic climate is highly favorable to Christianity" (Tocqueville 1955, 7).

This rosy assessment is based on two interrelated factors. Tocqueville argued that a natural, instinctive desire for immortality will always make a free man religious. This desire is based on two somewhat contradictory instincts: a fear of death and a dissatisfaction with life arising from an unbridgeable gap between imagined and attainable goods. "These different instincts," he remarks, "constantly drive his soul toward contemplation of the next world, and it is religion that leads him thither. Religion, therefore, is only one particular form of hope, and it is as natural to the human heart as hope itself" (296–297, 300, 535).

Tocqueville also suggests that Christianity is congenial to democracy because of its commitment to equality. Thus, when the religion is faithful to its values, it is not likely to encounter political opposition. This is true even for the Catholic Church which requires complete submission to its authority in matters of faith. Although the Pope rules like an absolute monarch and the priests are raised above the people, all others, regardless of their social or economic standing, are absolutely equal before the altar (288).

Tocqueville's more extended explanation for the mutual hostility between French liberals and Christians, however, casts doubt on this optimistic assessment.

Here he traces this ill will to the period of history known as the Enlightenment, which he linked to the spread of the social condition of equality. The Enlightenment was based on a philosophical method which made private, rational judgment the "most apparent and accessible test of truth" (430). Rationalists tend to reject imposed systems of thought, all forms of traditional authority, and all claims based on the extraordinary or the super-natural (429–430).

The philosophical method first appeared on history's stage in the sixteenth century when common people began to enjoy some of the tangible benefits of the democratic revolution. As democracy spread, this new way of thinking traveled in its wake, insidiously under-mining established institutions. In the seventeenth cen-tury, Bacon in the natural sciences and Descartes in speculative philosophy used this method to destroy "the dominion of tradition" and to overthrow the "authority of masters." In the eighteenth century, the French *philosophes* inaugurated the Enlightenment by arguing that everyone had an equal capacity to discern the truth about all matters, including religion and govern-ment (431).

The influence of the Enlightenment spread dramati-cally as the pace of the democratic revolution quick-ened. By the early nineteenth century, the philosophic method had become the "common coin of thought" in both Europe and America giving the universal right of private judgment a hallowed place in the pantheon of democratic values (431). Tocqueville thought most sub-jects far too complex to yield their truths to private individuals. He was convinced, however, that reliance on private judgment was a permanent feature of demo-cratic life, a feature with which statesmen seeking to promote religion and freedom would always have to contend (434, 615).

Tocqueville believed that the ascendence of enlightenment rationalism made the task of insuring
Christianity's survival in democracy highly problematic.
All forms of traditional Christianity are based on theological systems, on some form of hierarchy, and on
faith in the supernatural. While democrats, like most
individuals, naturally yearn for the security these religions provide, their enlightened habits of mind tend to
make them skeptics (434). As Tocqueville points out,
the democratic "spirit of individual independence" is
religion's "most dangerous enemy" (449). Freedom requires religion, but skepticism endangers it.

THE LESSONS OF FRENCH HISTORY

Tocqueville believed that the chief task of religious
statesmanship in modern times was to protect Christianity and freedom against the tides of democratic skepticism. French statesmen and churchmen in the eighteenth and early nineteenth centuries failed in this
regard because they could not respond adequately to
the changes in public opinion wrought by the Enlightenment. The Catholic clergy erred by supporting their
country's historic alliance between church and state at
a time when this alliance clashed with emerging notions of democratic freedom (Tocqueville 1955, 148–
157). French liberals erred by attributing the corruptions
of the Church in the Old Regime to Christianity itself
while failing to appreciate Christianity's political usefulness (17).

Tocqueville considered church–state alliances harmful to religion at all times. Whenever a religion accepts
political support, it weakens its natural hold over the
human soul. An established church must defend its
patron's interests and oppose its adversaries even when
such actions alienate its would be friends. "Religion

cannot share the material strength of the rulers," he noted, "without being burdened with some of the animosity roused against them" (297). More important, it may be forced to defend political principles contrary to its own (297–298).

In aristocratic times, church–state alliances are generally functional because the people are passive and consider the existing social and political order sacred, immortal, and beyond reproach. The danger to religion from such alliances exists, but it is neither imminent nor obvious. As societies become more democratic, this danger becomes more visible, but less manageable. These societies are agitated and unstable, and partisanship and changes in public opinion weaken their long-standing institutions. Established religion is especially vulnerable under such circumstances. "Linked to ephemeral powers," Tocqueville muses, "it follows their fortunes and often falls together with the passions of a day sustaining them" (298).

Such was the case in France. As long as France remained an aristocratic, monarchical society "immobility and somnolence" was the rule and little threatened its government (298). Despite Christianity's commitment in principle to equal freedom, the French Church was an integral part of the Old Regime, giving its moral support to the monarchy and embracing its aristocratic principles. In return, the government delegated considerable responsibility over secular affairs to the Church. Clergymen were lords of the manors, landed proprietors, and tax collectors, as well as occupants of the most powerful and privileged positions in the French government. The Church flourished as long as obedience to traditional authority governed French society, but ensured its own demise when it failed to adapt to the gradual democratization of mores (Tocqueville 1955, 151–152).

The *philosophes* were the chief agents of change in pre-revolutionary France, attacking and ridiculing the irrationalities and injustices of the Old Regime in the name of reason and private judgment. They assaulted the Catholic Church with "a sort of studious ferocity" and undermined the "very foundations of Christian belief" (Tocqueville 1955, 6). During the government's waning days, a large portion of the then useless and largely impotent aristocracy adopted their irreligious ideas and spread them among the masses. This enlightened elite generally believed that Christianity was inimical to liberty and therefore had to be destroyed (Tocqueville 1955, 154–155).

But it was ultimately less for religious than for concrete political reasons that the *philosophes* attacked the Church so vehemently. The French authors who assaulted the government were censured and harassed by the Church and thus had "almost personal" reasons for opposing religion (Tocqueville 1955, 151). In addition, the Church was seen as the most vulnerable and least defended part of the Old Regime. The powers of the Church had diminished as those of the secular authority increased, and the French monarchy showed much less zeal in defending the faith than in safeguarding its own interests (Tocqueville 1955, 152). When the attacks reached their peak, no one defended the religion. Those who remained Christians kept silent, fearing ostracism more than heresy, and even the Church itself seemed ready to "repudiate the faith for which she stood" (Tocqueville 1955, 154–155).

The decisive reason for the downfall of the Church, however, was its continuing link to the social condition of inequality while the whole fabric of aristocracy was crumbling. "The real object of the Revolution," Tocqueville wrote, "was less a new form of government than a new form of society" (Tocqueville 1959, 160).

Because the public identified the Church with the Old Regime and perceived both as enemies of democratic freedom, they fell together beneath the irreversible tide of the democratic revolution.

Tocqueville considered the early period of the French Revolution a glorious epoch in human history and admired its statesmen for their self-confidence, idealism, and heroism (Tocqueville 1955, 156). In the last analysis, though, he thought their anti-Christian policies a failure of statecraft which produced dire political consequences. When the Revolution first shook France's Christian foundations, it created a metaphysical vacuum. The ensuing chaos and confusion quickly led to the rise of a new "species of religion," a "political gospel" whose core principle was atheism and whose every idea resembled a dogma (Tocqueville 1955, 13; Tocqueville 1959, 101). Unlike the elite atheisms of the past, the new "political gospel" deeply affected the masses. "Its secular doctrines were not only believed," Tocqueville noted, "but ardently preached, an entirely new thing in history" (Tocqueville 1959, 102).

Tocqueville considered this "political gospel" strangely similar to Christianity in many respects. It had required beliefs, a universal moral order based on egalitarian principles, and its own "apostles, militants, and martyrs" who sought to regenerate the human race (Tocqueville 1955, 12–13). In contrast to Christianity, however, it lacked an otherworldly support for virtue and for the higher human aspirations and decencies (Tocqueville 1955, 13). These aberrations destroyed the moral boundaries separating liberty from license, fostered a deadly strain of political utopianism, and brought to the fore a "hitherto unknown breed" of men who shamelessly trampled on the people's rights in their own name (Tocqueville 1955, 157; Tocqueville 1959, 162).

Thus in the end, the Christian statesmen who sided with the Old Regime to strengthen Christianity and preserve their privileges helped bring about the French Revolution. The liberals who sought to promote freedom by cleansing France of Christian influence helped cause the terror and tyranny of the Revolution's later phases. These errors in judgment continued to haunt France in the post-Napoleonic era. The Bourbon attempts to reestablish the Catholic Church exacerbated the anticlericalism of the liberals, making religion a strictly partisan affair in their eyes (Goldstein 1975, 32). Seeing the Church in the "ranks of their adversaries," they either attacked it openly or failed to defend it (17). The Church, on the other hand, came once again "to rebuff the equality which it loves and to abuse freedom as its adversary" (17).

CONCLUSION

Tocqueville thought the lessons of this sorry period in French history were crystal clear. Liberal statesmen must learn to appreciate Christianity's political value and strengthen it in every way possible. At the very least, this requires religious disestablishment so that faith can draw on its natural strength without becoming embroiled in divisive political controversy. Committed Christians must forego political power, embrace the principles of liberal democracy, and somehow adapt their creeds to enlightenment rationalism. Finally, each side must recognize its dependence on the other and make common ground against inflexible allies.

Unfortunately, Tocqueville did not live to realize his hope for a productive partnership between liberals and traditionalists in France.[6] When he retired from political life at the beginning of the Second Empire, the Church was again using the throne to buttress its own strength and, as one scholar put it, "the sum total of public virtue displayed by most of the French clergy" was "subservience to an authoritarian state" (Goldstein 1975, 96). French liberals had also, by this time, long cast aside their tentative willingness to accommodate religion and were pursuing a wholly secular path (Goldstein 1975, 129).

CHAPTER FIVE

AMERICA'S RELIGIOUS HORIZON

For most people in the United States religion . . . is republican, for the truths of the other world are held subject to private judgment. . . . Each man is allowed to choose freely the path that will lead him to heaven. . . . (397).

Tocqueville's Americans were practically oriented, averse to general ideas, and indifferent to the intellectual battles raging between European rationalists and traditionalists (302; see Ceasar 1990, 143–144). Yet America's democratic social condition led them naturally, by a kind of cultural osmosis, to adopt the basic premises of the European enlightenment. These were, as we have seen, that private judgment is sacrosanct, that the masses are educable, and that "nothing passes beyond the limits of intelligence" (430). Such beliefs made Americans worldly in outlook, optimistic in temperament, and convinced that popular enlightenment was both desirable and necessary.

Yet they had managed to accomplish what their French counterparts could not: they secured freedom by fostering religious belief and practice within a rationalist, skeptical milieu—and Tocqueville admired them for it. Tocqueville considered America of the 1830s the "most enlightened and the freest" country in the world as well as the "place where the Christian religion has kept the greatest real power over men's souls" (291). This power, he emphasized, was "not just that of a philosophy which has been examined and accepted, but that of a religion believed in without discussion" (432). In protecting Christianity against democratic skepticism, they seemed to refute the *philosophes* who predicted that religious zeal would die down as freedom and enlightenment spread (295).

My task in this chapter is to explain how America achieved this happy combination of religion, enlightenment, and freedom. Tocqueville attributes America's success in promoting religion to four interrelated factors. The first was America's Puritan origins which made Christianity an integral part of our national character (432). The second was America's good fortune in escaping the destructive and disorienting effects of a social revolution. In this respect America's democratic history was far more benign than that of France. The third was America's capacity to appreciate the usefulness of religion to freedom (432–433). Indeed, the "ideas of Christianity and liberty" were "so completely mingled" in the minds of most Americans that it was "almost impossible to get them to conceive of one without the other" (293).

The fourth, and most important, was America's commitment to the separation of church and state (295).[1] As we shall see, each of these factors in its own way helped transform traditional American Protestantism into an anthropocentric religion with enlightenment roots. This more "civil" version of the faith enjoyed the overwhelming support of American public opinion, but achieved this support only by sacrificing its transcendent principles.

AMERICA'S FOUNDING AND ITS AMBIGUITIES

Tocqueville begins his analysis of American religion by turning to America's founding, a subject he considered central to his exegesis of our country's life. "There is not an opinion, custom, or law, nor one might add, an event, [in American life]," he asserts "which the point of departure will not easily explain" (32). He also thought his discussion distinguished his "new political science" from its predecessors. While the "old" political science recognized the importance of founding, it lacked, in his view, the sound historical evidence needed to pierce the veil of ignorance surrounding the origins of nations. Thus, the "first causes" of national life were forever beyond its ken (32). America's founders enabled Tocqueville to understand their accomplishments by leaving to history a "faithful record of their opinions, mores, and laws" (32). Tocqueville believed his study of this legacy made him the first political scientist to be "exact about the influence of the point of departure on the future of a state" (32).

Tocqueville suggests at various points in the *Democracy* that the Puritans decisively shaped American life by making Christian piety the dominant element in our national character (47, 291, 432).[2] Religion shaped American mores in the 1830s, he wrote, reigning "without obstacles, by universal consent," and extending its sway over reason itself (292). Tocqueville's claims should not, however, be taken at face value. A close examination of the *Democracy* shows that, in his view, the "strict puritanism [sic]" of colonial America was already "much relaxed" by Jackson's time (712). Indeed, Tocqueville wrote to his close friend, Louis de Kergolay in 1831 that America's once strong religious impulse was "expiring day by day" (Tocqueville 1985, 48; Tocqueville 1951–, 13(1):227). As we shall see, he also shows the careful reader that sexual morality, political life, and indeed, all significant elements of America's national character in Jackson's day had a secular rather than a religious foundation.

Tocqueville's most extended discussion of the Puritans appears in an early chapter of the *Democracy* entitled "Concerning Their Point of Departure and Its Importance for the Future of the Anglo-Americans" (31–49). This chapter, he tells us, provides the "key to almost the whole work" (32). He first suggests that an understanding of the Puritan experience in America will explain every aspect of America's mature national character just as knowledge of a baby's behavior will disclose the sum of its future personality. "The whole man is there . . . in the cradle," he asserts (31, 279).

In the chapter's epilogue, however, Tocqueville calls this analogy into question by remarking that it "was not open" to the Puritans "to found a society with no other point of departure besides themselves" (48). In contrast to an infant whose history begins at birth, the Puritans were self-conscious historical actors, completely civilized when they arrived in New England (302). In fact, as Tocqueville later observes, American society "had no infancy, being born adult" (303). Understanding Tocqueville's Puritans therefore, requires us to consider his account of the roots of Puritanism as well as his treatment of their history in America. Tocqueville does not discuss the origins of Puritanism directly, but he does elucidate these origins both in the "point of departure" chapter and in the *Democracy* as a whole.

Tocqueville also points to another, more serious problem with the analogy. If taken literally, it suggests that statesmen, moralists, and political philosophers like himself can have very little influence on a nation's character after its founding. Indeed, it seems to make Tocqueville a determinist who drastically downplays the role of rational deliberation and choice in politics and in adult life. But one of Tocqueville's main reasons for writing on politics was to oppose all explanations of human behavior which endanger freedom by denying its existence (544, 594–595, 705). One should never assume, he warns, that a nation's character is forever fixed. Within certain constraints, "each fresh generation is new material for the lawgiver to mold" (95, 163).

As Tocqueville describes it, Puritanism was a unique combination of the *spirit of religion* and the *spirit of freedom* (47). The primary source for the Puritan spirit of religion was the Old Testament. The great drama of that book culminates in God's deliverance of the Jews from Egypt, the revelation to Moses at Mt. Sinai, and the subsequent journey of the Chosen People to the Promised Land. Drawing on historical accounts, Tocqueville shows that these events provided the theological framework which shaped the Puritans' understanding of their own exodus from Europe, their perilous journey to America, their privileged status in God's eyes, and the founding of the New England colonies (36–37). Tocqueville also shows that biblical Judaism inspired the passion for orthodoxy and the respect for religious authority which fueled the Puritan spirit of religion (41–42).

The Puritan spirit of freedom had its roots in the New Testament and was strongly democratic. According to Tocqueville, Christ was the first historical figure to teach that all human beings had an "equal right . . . at birth to liberty," thus distinguishing Christianity from Judaism and pagan religion as we have seen (439; see above, pp. 48–49).

Tocqueville first suggests that the Puritans combined the spirit of religion and the spirit of freedom in a way both faithful to Christianity and suitable for founding America as a healthy Christian society (46, 47). He further implies that historical clashes between the two "spirits" were not the result of defects in Christianity, but rather of improper alliances between church and state, partisan distortions of the religion, or sincere errors regarding its nature (16, 17, 300, 301).

On a deeper level, though, Tocqueville shows that an inherent conflict within Christianity itself made the balance achieved by the Puritans unworkable over time. Put simply, the democratic revolution Christ set in motion was opposed in principle to certain key elements of ancient Judaism, creating an unstable situation which ultimately led the spirit of freedom to triumph over the spirit of religion in Christian theology, politics, and morals. I shall discuss the theological transformation wrought by the spirit of freedom in this chapter, the democratization of American politics in chapter 6, and America's moral revolution in chapter 7.

The spirit of freedom's first theological accomplishment was to liberate Christians from a host of legal obligations embodied in the Mosaic code. Early Christianity emphasized belief rather than behavior, restricting its moral precepts to the "general relations between man and God and between man and man" (445). The Catholic Church retained the Old Testament's requirement of strict submission to authority in theological matters, however, making itself the ultimate arbiter of religious duty. Martin Luther challenged Catholicism on this point, teaching that "all men are equally able to find the path to heaven" and that private judgment has a marginal role to play in discovering religious truth (11). This idea led Protestants to reject the Church's monopoly on Scriptural interpretation and to allow individuals to scrutinize some religious dogmas rationally (431).

Tocqueville considered this partial shift from an external to an internal source of doctrinal authority the beginning of a process which transformed Christianity from an otherworldly faith into a component of democratic public opinion. Luther's intent in pitting the individual against the Church's power was to establish the Bible as the sole source of Christian orthodoxy, thus insuring that God's will alone would be normative (Dillenberger and Welch 1954, 45–47).[3] In Tocqueville's view, however, Luther established a mixed regime in the Protestant soul, dividing sovereignty in religious matters between freedom and authority, reason and revelation, and ultimately the individual and God (450–451; Tocqueville 1985, 52; Tocqueville 1951–, 13(1): 230). But Tocqueville believed that mixed regimes are inherently unstable (251), and that, in the case of Protestantism, the instability doomed the faith. He states this conclusion most forcefully in a letter to Kergolay written shortly after he arrived in America:

> It seems clear to me that the reformed religion is a kind of compromise, a sort of *representative monarchy* in matters of religion which can well fill an era, serve as the passage from one state to another, but which cannot constitute a definitive state itself . . . and which is approaching an end" (Tocqueville 1985, 49–50; Tocqueville 1951–, 13(1):228 emphasis in text).

Tocqueville believed that American Protestantism exhibited the weaknesses of Protestantism generally and provided "precious information" regarding its future (Tocqueville 1985, 50; Tocqueville 1951–, 13(1):228). Its chief defect was its tendency to promote schism or division among Christians over doctrinal matters. Schism was responsible for America's birth. The first Puritans were Protestant reformers who remained within the Anglican Church after its break with Rome, but sought to purify or purge it of its Catholic elements. The New England Puritans migrated to America during the 1630s

when their religious–political situation at home was particularly harsh. In these years, some twenty thousand
people came to New England and established colonies
at Massachusetts Bay, Connecticut, New Haven, and
Rhode Island (Vaughan 1972, xi–xv, 1, 2, 65, 297;
Ahlstrom 1972, chapters 6, 8, and 9).

At first, schism reinforced the zealotry that produced it. It was the Puritans' theological quarrel with
Anglicanism that fueled the passion for orthodoxy which
led them to forsake European comforts for the "inevitable sufferings of exile" (36). Tocqueville admired the
heroism, nobility of spirit, and commitment to freedom
this religious idealism inspired. He was considerably
less positive, though, about its fanatical tendencies
which he held responsible for the intolerance and moral
extremism that marred New England life (42–43).

In the long run, however, schism fragmented American Protestantism, fatally weakening its capacity to
nourish faith. Tocqueville saw an "innumerable multitude" of Protestant sects in America, but credited Protestantism with little real power (290; Tocqueville, 1985,
50; Tocqueville 1951–, 13(1):229). Doubt was the source
of this growing weakness. It is hard, Tocqueville observed, for a thinking person to believe in his own orthodoxy when surrounded by a cacophony of dissenting
voices. Indeed, under such circumstances, Tocqueville
writes, it is "almost as easy to assume that there is no
religion as that there are several" (450).

Tocqueville's Luther also contributed to the demise
of traditional Christianity in a less direct, less well known
way. By providing a small opening for private, rational
judgment in religious matters, he founded the philosophical method, or way of thinking, which eventually
made the individual the starting point for all forms of
intellectual inquiry (430–431). It was this method which
gave birth to the Enlightenment, destroyed the Catholic

Church in France, and led to the atheism of the French Revolution. "The selfsame spirit," Tocqueville wrote, "that in Luther's day had led several million Catholics to break away from the mother church incited others, year by year, to go still further and to repudiate Christianity altogether; thus after heresy came unbelief" (Tocqueville 1955, 148).

Tocqueville first suggests that American Protestantism resisted the Enlightenment more successfully than French Catholicism by establishing religious autonomy for the individual without compromising religions's authority. He shows, however, that by the 1830s the individual rather than the Bible was, at least in theory, the final arbiter of religious truth (66, 373–374, 397). By accommodating to this basic principle of the Enlightenment, American religious reformers conceded more to reason and private judgment than the Puritans or any traditional Protestants would have allowed.

JEFFERSON AND ENLIGHTENMENT CHRISTIANITY

The greatest of these reformers was Thomas Jefferson, the man Tocqueville considered the "most powerful apostle of democracy there has ever been" (261). Tocqueville carefully read Jefferson's *Notes on the State of Virginia* and a selection of his letters in 1833 and 1834 and made at least twenty-one specific references to him in the texts and manuscripts of the first half of the *Democracy* (Schleifer 1991, 178). Historian James T. Schleifer points to direct links between Jefferson's writings and Tocqueville's views on equality, his fascination with inheritance laws, his account of the American Revolution, his analysis of the legislative and judicial branches of American government, and his discussions of American Indians and blacks (Schleifer 1991, 178–179).

There are no references in Tocqueville's writings, however, to Jefferson's work as a religious reformer.[4] As a result, we cannot know for certain whether Tocqueville was aware of this work or considered it significant. We can say with some confidence however that Jefferson met all of Tocqueville's criteria for successful religious statesmanship in democratic times. This fact justifies a brief discussion of his religious–political thought and accomplishments.

Jefferson was nominally an Anglican (Ahlstrom 1972, 376). In his public and private writings on Christianity, however, he discredited Anglicanism and all other forms of Christian orthodoxy by arguing that God's favor depends not on the "rightness," but the "uprightness" or sincerity of one's beliefs (Jefferson 1944, 433). Jefferson's defense of this principle contributed significantly to the growth of what scholars today call "religious individualism" (Roof and McKinney 1987, 32). A religious individualist holds that all people's religious views are equally valid, regardless of their content, because there is no objectively verifiable religious truth.[5]

We can gauge the extent of Jefferson's deviation from traditional Christianity by comparing his notion of the role of private, rational judgment in determining belief with that of the Puritans. For the Puritans, as for all traditional Protestants, the Bible was the ultimate religious authority, the touchstone for human affairs. The Puritans thought that each individual should read the Bible and rationally strive to understand it correctly. They also thought that reason should be used by clergy and laymen alike to evaluate and defend differing interpretations of Scripture. These views were responsible for the strong Puritan commitment to public education and the austere, argumentative intellectuality which characterized Puritan culture (33, 45; see Ahlstrom 1972, 130, and Vaughan 1972, 234).

No Puritan ever challenged the authority of the Bible on rational grounds, however. To do so would have been to subordinate the divine will to that of the individual, to raise the self above God, the most grievous Christian sin. Putting "carnal reason" above the "wisdom of the Lord," noted Puritan Thomas Hooker, dispossessed "God of that absolute supremacy which is indeed His prerogative royal." The punishment for a "poor insolent worm" guilty of such a crime was to be "pash[ed] to powder" and sent "packing to the pit every moment" (Hooker 1956, 155, 157).

Jefferson's views on the role of private, rational judgment in theological matters appear in a letter he wrote in 1787 to his nephew, Peter Carr, instructing him on how to approach religion (Jefferson 1944, 429–435, especially 431–433). In this letter, Jefferson asserts that reason rather than revelation is the appropriate standard for measuring religious beliefs. In examining the subject of religion, he advises Carr, a careful student must divest himself of "all bias in favor of novelty and singularity of opinion" as well as "all the fears and servile prejudices under which weak minds are servilely crouched." "Every fact, every opinion," he continued, is to be brought before the bar of reason (Jefferson 1944, 431). Indeed, as he later put it in a letter to Miles King, Jefferson thought that the truth or falsity of revelation itself must be determined by the individual:

> Whether the particular revelation which you suppose to have been made to yourself were real or imaginary, your reason alone is the competent judge. For dispute as long as we will on religious tenets, our reason at last must ultimately decide, as it is the only oracle which God has given us to determine between what really comes from Him and the phantasms of a disordered or deluded imagination (Jefferson 1905, 14:197)

Jefferson incorporated this theological position in his "Bill for Establishing Religious Freedom" written in 1779 and passed in a modified form by the Virginia legislature in 1786.[6] This Bill, which he considered one of the three greatest accomplishments of his political life, served as the prototype for the religion clauses of the First Amendment to the Constitution (Jefferson 1944, ii). In addition to disestablishing religion and establishing religious freedom, the Bill asserts that God seeks to extend religion not by force, or even by faith, but rather "by its influence on reason alone" (Jefferson 1950–, 2:545–547 emphasis in text). This novel conception of the deity was the centerpiece of a "rational" version of Christianity which Jefferson set forth in private writings and correspondence (see Kessler 1983a, 246–252).

For the Puritans, as for all traditional Protestants, religious freedom existed only to discover the one, correct path to salvation and to establish biblical commonwealths based on that path. The Puritans' concern for orthodoxy led them to establish religious uniformity within these commonwealths and to persecute dissenters. While church and state were nominally separate in Puritan America, government rigorously enforced religious and moral conformity (41–43). Certain of the truth, they felt that coercion in religious matters was an act of Christian charity. "Hypocrites give God part of his due, the outward man," wrote John Cotton, "but the profane person giveth God neither the outward nor the inward man" (cited in Vaughan 1972, 203). If sincerity is the chief criterion for salvation, as Jefferson suggests, however, then religious coercion in any form is sinful and Christians must be tolerant in both spirit and practice.

Tocqueville considered the separation of church and state the primary cause of Christianity's hold on America of the 1830s. During his visit here, he met "nobody, lay or cleric," who did not extol its virtues (295). Its chief virtue in his eyes was to give Americans the freedom to follow their natural inclinations, both religious and democratic. By "diminishing the apparent power of religion," he remarks, Americans have "increased its real strength" (296). He shows, however, that democrats, when free, are not likely to seek membership in the City of God. While their natural desire for immortality leads them to religion, their skepticism permits them to embrace only those faiths which require no sacrifice of their secular dispositions.

Jefferson, who shared Tocqueville's sense of America's underlying secularism, predicted that over time, most of his countrymen would become Unitarians (Jefferson 1944, 704). Unitarianism was the form of Christianity most closely akin to his "rational" version of the faith and most consistent with what Tocqueville reports as the democratic desire for religious unity and simplicity (445). Although Unitarianism was never as popular in America as Jefferson hoped or thought it would be, Tocqueville shows that by the 1830s, most Americans had accepted Jefferson's basic religious orientation:

> For most people in the United States religion . . . is republican, for the truths of the other world are held subject to private judgment, just as in politics the care for men's temporal interests is left to the good sense of all. Each man is allowed to choose freely the path that will lead him to heaven, just as the law recognizes each citizen's right to choose his own government (397).

While America's republican religion was Christian in name, it was opposed in principle to all forms of traditional Christianity and wholly consistent with the basic premises of the Enlightenment.

RELIGIOUS INDIFFERENCE AND THE REIGN OF AMERICAN PUBLIC OPINION

Although Tocqueville subtly points to the changes which took place in American Christianity between the seventeenth and nineteenth centuries, he neither highlights these changes nor directly explains why they occurred. He does elucidate them indirectly, though, when analyzing the phenomenon of religious indifference (see Manent 1982, 126–127). As we have seen, one source of this indifference, at least in America, was the Protestant tendency toward schism. Indifference also arises, Tocqueville observes, when people's beliefs are "silently undermined" by negative doctrines which "assert the falseness of one religion but do not establish the truth of any other" (299). One such doctrine, of course, is the view that divine revelation is spurious.

If such doctrines challenge traditional faith in revolutionary times as they did in late eighteenth-century France, they can swiftly triumph (644). When the challenge occurs in a peaceful epoch, however, it can gradually transform the mind without "the apparent cooperation of the passions of man and almost without his knowledge" (299, 640, 644). Such was the case in America, which embraced the Enlightenment but escaped the ravages of the democratic revolution (432). As American democracy matured, religious individualism gradually supplanted the metaphysical underpinnings of traditional Christianity and changed its external trappings in important respects.

Jefferson hoped his version of religious freedom would enable enlightened, autonomous adults to arrive at their own conclusions regarding the first and last things. Tocqueville shows, however, that this hope was as ill-founded as Luther's hope that some private judgment in religious matters would strengthen biblical authority. Virtually no human beings, Tocqueville thought, could answer weighty metaphysical questions for themselves, enlightenment claims notwithstanding. Thus, the need for certainty in religious matters forced almost everyone to accept some principle of authority on trust and without discussion. The critical questions Tocqueville asked when assessing American religious attitudes was not whether Americans deferred to religious authority, but "where it resides," "what its limits are," and whether the "bondage" was "salutary" (434, 435).

Tocqueville concluded that most Americans vested religious authority neither in God nor the self, but in democratic public opinion. "All the clergy of America are aware of the intellectual domination of the majority," he observed in the *Democracy*, "and they treat it with respect."

> They never struggle against it unless the struggle is necessary. They keep aloof from party squabbles, but they freely adopt the general views of their time and country and let themselves go unresistingly with the tide of feeling and opinion which carries everything around them along with it (449).

PUBLIC OPINION AND AMERICAN PROTESTANTISM

This deference to public opinion reshaped American Protestantism in a number of significant ways. Most Protestant clergymen deferred to the majority rather than to the founders of their faiths in matters involving theology, worship, and religious duty.[7] Perhaps the most basic of these accommodations concerned the priority given to religious belief. Traditional Protestants considered correct dogmatic belief the most important component of a good Christian life. "Not by the doing of works,"

Luther wrote, "but by believing do we glorify God and acknowledge that he is truthful" (Luther 1957, 31:353). This emphasis on belief fueled the Puritan passion for orthodoxy and led to the passage of laws which promoted it. The Connecticut criminal code was typical in this regard. The first provision of this code, drawn directly from "Holy Writ," revealed the depth of Puritan intolerance. "If any man after legal conviction," it read, "shall have or worship any other God but the Lord God, he shall be put to death" (41). The force of the law also fell on dissident groups "who chose to worship the same God with a ritual other than their own" (42, 43, notes 26, 27).

In Tocqueville's America, the Protestant clergy downplayed belief vis-à-vis good works so as not to offend the various sects whose articles of faith differed from their own. "Enter the churches . . . ," Tocqueville wrote to Kergolay, "and you hear them speak of morality; of dogma not a word, nothing that could in any way shock a neighbor, nothing that could reveal the hint of dissidence" (450; Tocqueville 1985, 49, 51; Tocqueville 1951–, 13(1): 228–230).

This emphasis on works in a free religious environment contributed significantly to America's high level of religious toleration which Tocqueville illustrated in a colorful, unpublished essay entitled "Sects in America" (Schleifer 1975, 248–254).[8] Here he recounts his experiences visiting Quaker and Methodist religious services in an unnamed American town. The Quakers, distinguished by their clothes, the gentleness of their spirit, and the silence of their worship, were worlds apart from the noisy and emotional Methodists (Schleifer 1975, 250–252). In the 1650s the Quakers obstructed the services of the Puritans who in turn persecuted them (42, 43, n. 26). In Tocqueville's day, however, the Quakers coexisted peacefully with their more traditional

Christian brethren, their churches separated by no more than a stone's throw.

In the 1830s, most Americans looked askance at supernatural claims, thinking that "everything in the world can be explained and that nothing passes beyond the limits of intelligence" (430). This skepticism led the majority to reject any intellectual or moral authority "beyond and outside humanity" (435). Most Protestant churches downplayed the miraculous and providential elements of their traditional faiths in deference to these attitudes. These churches also dispensed with any formalities and complicated religious practices offensive to the democratic spirit. "I have seen no country," Tocqueville noted, "in which Christianity is less clothed in forms, symbols, and observances than it is in the United States, or where the mind is fed with clearer, simpler, or more comprehensive conceptions" (448).

All traditional Christians conceived it a duty to subordinate self-interest to the common good and, above all, to God's will (see, for example, Vaughan 1972, 138–146). In the 1830s, most Americans notoriously neglected this duty, making their own self-interest paramount in every important respect (530). Rather than condemning self-interest, most American clergymen encouraged their congregations to be religious for selfish reasons. This concession extended especially to the strong American taste for material well-being. Although the New Testament teaches that a seeker of "treasures upon earth" can "hardly enter the kingdom of heaven," American churchmen respected and even supported the American preoccupation with wealth (Matthew 6:19, 19:23). They took an active interest in the progress of commerce and industry, pointed to the links between temporal and spiritual prosperity, and criticized only those who became rich dishonestly. Indeed, it was "often difficult to be sure when listening" to these churchmen, Tocqueville noted, "whether the main object of religion is to preserve eternal felicity in the next world or prosperity in this" (449, 529, 530).

Tocqueville first suggests that American Protestantism's accommodations to majority opinion involved "secondary notions," and not the "chief opinions" of the faith which remained inviolate (447). Traditional Protestantism taught, however, that God rules the universe, that faith or belief takes precedence over works, and that miracles, divine revelation, and divine providence are irrefutable facts. In giving up, or at least deemphasizing these doctrines, American Protestants compromised essential as well as secondary things (436).

Tocqueville thought that these changes brought a grievous loss to real Christianity, drastically reducing its power over the American soul. "Religion does not move . . . [Americans] . . . deeply," he noted in his letter to Kergolay. Very few American Protestants made the sacrifices of time, effort, and wealth for the faith that one would expect from the truly pious nor did they seem to fear otherwordly punishment. Rather, they followed their religion "the way our fathers took a medicine in the month of May—if it does not do any good, people seem to say, at least it cannot do any harm" (Tocqueville 1985, 49; Tocqueville 1951–, 13(1):228). This indifference made Christians who "follow[ed] their habits rather than their convictions" and hypocrisy was common. Ultimately, Tocqueville could not determine just how many American Protestants sincerely believed, "for who can read the secrets of the heart" (291, 293)?

THE CORE OF AMERICAN FAITH

If most Americans were no longer traditional Protestants, what did they believe in? What were the first principles that enabled them to act in a coherent and rational manner? Tocqueville subtly shows that by conforming so extensively to public opinion, American Protestants replaced their God-oriented faith for a new "sort of religion" in which equality was God and the majority the lawgiver (435–436).

Tocqueville describes this new sort of religion at various points in the *Democracy*. Its core beliefs, zealously held, were that the people are sovereign, that they have the right to determine religious truth for themselves, that their capacities for this task are roughly equal, and that truth, therefore, "will be found on the side of the majority" (397, 435). Its secondary notions include the ideas that happiness can be attained without God, that self-interest is honorable if "properly understood," and that humanity as a whole is capable of indefinite improvement (453, 525). These beliefs made Americans, for the most part, thisworldly rather than otherworldly, proud rather than humble, selfish rather than altruistic and rational rather than pious.

Tocqueville shows that for most Americans faith in public opinion was more psychologically satisfying than faith in either traditional Protestantism or in enlightenment rationalism. The majority in America supplied the faithful with a "quantity of ready-made opinions," thereby relieving them of an unsustainable intellectual burden and its accompanying doubt (435).[9] The faithful, in turn, "place[d] almost unlimited confidence in the judgment of the public" and proudly claimed its opinions as their own (435). In the last analysis, however, they were less concerned with the content of these opinions than with their social acceptability.

Ironically, Americans paid for their membership in public opinion's church with true religious freedom, that is the freedom of nonconformity (see Manent 1982, 130–131). Eschewing argument and persuasion, the majority compelled belief "by some mighty pressure of the mind of all upon the intelligence of each" (435). Resistance to this pressure, which entered into the very depths of the soul, was virtually impossible. In democracy, Tocqueville notes, it is "very difficult for a man to believe what the mass rejects and to profess what it condemns" (643).

Tocqueville thought that, appearances notwithstanding, there was more true religious freedom in Europe than in America of the 1830s. Although most European countries had religious establishments, their mixed social structures gave refuge and encouragement to the dissenter. "In democratic countries the aristocracy . . . support[ed] him, and in other lands the democracy" (255). In Tocqueville's America, however, there was "only one authority, one source of strength and of success, and nothing outside it" (255). Although the majority didn't banish or burn heretics, it silenced them more effectively by ostracism (255–256).[10] Luther himself, Tocqueville notes, probably would have been denied a hearing under these circumstances (642).

Tocqueville's greatest fear was that, over time, majority opinion would snuff out both the remembrance of traditional faith and the prospects for religious innovation. As strong, independent thinkers vanished from the American scene, less hardy souls could very well give up thinking altogether (435–436). Tocqueville's survey of the American religious horizon did little to allay his fears. Despite the high level of religious activity, he found "less independence of mind and true freedom of discussion" here than in any other country familiar to him (254–255). Ironically, the same democratic forces which fostered enlightenment rationalism and Protestant sectarianism threatened in the 1830s to "confine the activity of private judgment within limits too narrow for the dignity and happiness of mankind" (436).

Americans also paid a steep price in happiness for their worship of equality. Traditional Christians repressed "a crowd of petty passing desires" for the sake of salvation and could be happy in their faith even if not prosperous, enlightened, or free (547–548). Tocqueville's Americans, in contrast, were prosperous, enlightened, and free, but not really happy. "A cloud habitually hung on their brow," he observed, "and they seemed serious and almost sad even in their pleasures" (536). In his mind, this restless melancholy was due largely to a virtual abandonment of otherworldly hopes (536).[11]

> A man who has set his heart on nothing but the good things of this world is always in a hurry, for he has only a limited time in which to find them, get them, and enjoy them. Remembrance of the shortness of life continually goads him on. Apart from the goods he has, he thinks of a thousand others which death will prevent him from tasting if he does not hurry. This thought fills him with distress, fear, and regret and keeps his mind continually in agitation . . . (536–537).

Tocqueville's argument regarding America's faith in the majority requires a reassessment of his claim that American Protestantism in his day exercised "real power over men's souls" (291). As we have seen, Protestantism *was* powerful in America, but "less as a revealed doctrine than as part of common opinion" (436). As such, its traditional doctrines cohabited uneasily with the majority's secular beliefs, giving ground in cases of conflict. No Protestant church in the 1830s could seriously teach the propriety of religious persecution or any other traditional doctrine contrary to egalitarianism's "chief opinions." Although it could dispute certain "secondary notions" of the majority's faith, its arguments would most probably fall on deaf ears. No exhortations about original sin, for example, were likely to shake the majority's rosy assessment of human nature.

The loss American Protestants sustained in this arrangement was apparent only to the discerning observer (300). In exchange for the sacrifices public opinion exacted from Christianity, it loved, supported, and honored the faith (300). It also required all Americans to attend to the proprieties—to go to church, to profess belief outwardly, and to respect the Sabbath, which, Tocqueville remarked, was observed "Judaically" (p. 291, 295, 300, 542; Tocqueville 1985, 48; Tocqueville 1951, 13(1):227). Thus, the Puritan legacy continued to exert a profound influence on America's national character. The Christian spirit of freedom ultimately led Americans unconsciously to worship public opinion when private, rational judgment proved incapable of satisfying their metaphysical needs. While the Christian spirit of religion no longer acted independently on the America soul, its residual influence on public opinion left the country, at least in appearance, the most Christian nation in the world (291, but see 449).

AMERICAN CATHOLICISM AS A MODEL FOR FRANCE

Tocqueville paid special attention to American Catholicism in the *Democracy*, devoting key chapters to discussing its character, its progress, and its political efficacy. This is odd, as Cynthia J. Hinckley points out, because of the Church's minority status in America and Tocqueville's repeated assertions that Puritanism shaped the country's character (Hinckley 1990a, 327). Tocqueville's rhetorical strategy here, however, is easy to discern. His primary motive for studying American religion was to benefit France (Hinckley 1990a, 325). As we have seen, he wished to show his French compatriots that Catholicism and liberal democracy were not as incompatible as France's current imbroglio suggested. Likewise, his recommendations for preserving religion in democracy were meant primarily for French ears.

The gist of this advice, as we have seen, was that churchmen remain "studiously aloof" from "worldly business" while compromising with the majority in matters "not contrary to faith" (448). Such are the requirements of a skeptical age where majority public opinion is the "first" and most "irresistible" of powers (448). His particular message to French Catholics in all this was quite clear. For their church to survive, it must separate itself from day to day politics, deemphasize if not eliminate the worship of saints and other secondary agents, trim its minor rituals, and respect the passion for well-being which gripped the French bourgeoisie (445–448; Hinckley 1990a, 333–338).

Tocqueville also admonished the Church to hold fast to its core beliefs regardless of the spirit of the age (447). This warning, however, must be taken with a grain of salt. The main goal of traditional Christianity, both Catholic and Protestant, was to lead people toward eternal salvation through faith in God. If democratic majorities are predominantly secular, if they always establish belief, and if "no force" outside them can "support a prolonged resistance," then even the essential must bend in order for French Catholicism to thrive (448).

Tocqueville drives home his recommendations to his French audience by describing the benign effects of accommodationism on the Catholic Church in America, a church he knew well because of his intimate acquaintance with several American priests (297). In the 1830s, American Catholicism was flourishing. It boasted more than a million members, products of the Irish immigration of the late eighteenth century and of a significant proselytizing effort. These Catholics were full of ardor and zeal for their beliefs, and, according to all indications, were increasing prodigously (288; Tocqueville 1985, 50; see also Ahlstrom 1972, ch. 33).

Tocqueville attributed the strength of American Catholicism to several factors. The first, and perhaps most important, was the Church's strict adherence to the principle of separation between church and state (295). In some cases law, and in all cases public opinion, prohibited the mixing of the two. Catholic priests voluntarily shunned political power, taking "a sort of professional pride in claiming that it was no concern of theirs" (296). Thus, they held no public appointments or elective offices, and were "careful to keep clear of all parties, shunning contact with them with all the anxiety attendant upon personal interest" (296).[12]

The American clergy also allowed their congregations full freedom with regard to public affairs. While railing against political opinions which served as a cloak for ambition and bad faith, they taught that God valued sincerity of political expression and that in matters of government "it is no more a sin to make a mistake . . . than it is a sin to go wrong in building one's house or plowing one's field" (296). This attitude toward politics was partly the result of legal prohibitions, partly the result of the Church's minority status, and partly the result of public pressure. American public opinion tolerated no partisanship from any religious figure (289, 296).

The second factor was the Church's adherence to the basic principles of the American regime. In contrast to the French Catholics who supported the Old Regime, American Catholicism formed "the most republican and democratic of all classes in the United States" (288). In this respect, they were faithful to Christ's doctrine that all human beings have an "equal right . . . at birth to liberty" (439). Tocqueville also suggests that the Church's structure is compatible with equality. Although the Pope rules like an absolute monarch and the priests are raised above the people, all others, regardless of their social or economic standing, are absolutely equal before the altar. Indeed, all human beings are subject to the same standards in matters of dogma, details of belief, observances, and austerities (288).

Finally, Catholicism's requirement of complete submission to religious authority has a strong, although covert, appeal for democrats. While equality causes people to reject traditional religious authority, true freedom in religious matters is, as we have seen, spiritually debilitating and difficult for democrats to sustain. Catholicism appeals more to the senses than to the intellect and therefore seizes the democratic soul more deeply. While many of the Church's doctrines and customs astonish them, democrats feel a secret admiration for its discipline, its mysteries, and its extraordinary unity (450; Tocqueville 1985, 51).

Tocqueville believed that Catholicism had a much brighter future in France than Protestantism and never, therefore, recommended that France adopt America's dominant faith.[13] He was inherently conservative about religious matters and thought it foolhardy to tamper with any country's religious roots however frayed (544). He also believed, as we have just seen, that Catholicism was more capable of providing metaphysical certainty than Protestantism and therefore more useful to democracy in general. While he predicted that some Frenchmen would always choose to "let their minds float at random between obedience and freedom," he thought their number would be "fewer in democratic ages than at other times" (450–451). "Our grandchildren," he concluded, "will tend more and more to be divided clearly between those who have completely abandoned Christianity and those who have returned to the Church of Rome" (451).

Tocqueville's praise for American Catholicism did not, however, lead him to suggest that it could ever replace Protestantism as the dominant American faith. He considered this unlikely to occur for a number of reasons. Although some American Protestants were converting to Catholicism in the early nineteenth century, America's Protestant heritage was so much a part of the country's national character and American public opinion so conservative, that these conversions were not likely to seriously affect the Church's minority status (640). There was also a countervailing tendency for American Catholics to leave Christianity altogether. Thus, while Catholicism might continue to grow in America relative to other religious groups, it was likely to suffer considerable attrition in the future (450).

Tocqueville also indicates that the easy integration of Catholics into American society was connected in important ways to their minority status. American Catholics, in general, were more zealous than their Protestant counterparts and less inclined to accommodate to the prevailing ethos of religious relativism. "For them there is only truth in a single point," Tocqueville notes. "On any line one side or another of this point: eternal damnation" (Tocqueville 1985, 50; Tocqueville, 1951–, 13(1):229). Indeed, Tocqueville suggests that their respect for religious freedom, and for democratic principles in general, was due more to their social position and small numbers than to the true nature of their beliefs. If the Church ever did become wealthy and powerful in America, he implies, its hidden political ambitions and natural penchant for intolerance might arouse implacable hostility (289).

Finally, the democratic propensities which impelled American Protestantism to jettison the transcendent elements of its faith affected American Catholicism as well. American priests rejected the "petty individual observances," the "extraordinary and peculiar ways to salvation," the worship of saints, and other aspects of traditional Catholicism which offended the democratic ethos (449). More important, they, like their Protestant brethren, respected the intellectual dominion of the majority and never struggled against it unnecessarily. This led them to the same compromises with materialism and self-interest that so dramatically affected Protestantism (449). Although Catholicism had not, perhaps, become as completely governed by American public opinion as Protestantism during Tocqueville's time, it was certainly moving in that direction.

CONCLUSION

A brief recapitulation of this chapter is now in order. Tocqueville considered the Puritans America's founders and occasionally claimed that their orthodox form of Protestantism was the dominant American faith in the 1830s. He clearly showed, however, that over time the Puritan spirit of freedom helped transform biblical Protestantism into an anthropocentric faith. Building on an enlightenment version of this spirit, religious statesmen such as Thomas Jefferson made the individual rather than the Bible the ultimate source of religious authority in America and separated church from state. The more civil, tolerant, and diverse Christianities resulting from these changes earned the overwhelming support of American public opinion, but only by sacrificing their transcendent principles. Most Americans in the 1830s were wedded to this world despite their overt commitments to the biblical God.

Tocqueville considered America's "bondage" to Christianized public opinion "salutary," despite his fears for genuine religious freedom and genuine faith (434). In the end, he thought it highly unlikely that either could thrive in democracy's highly materialistic and skeptical environment. Thus, he praised American Protestantism and recommends a democratized version of Catholicism to France as its best hope for synthesizing reason and faith. Chapter 6 will consider Tocqueville's analysis of how such a synthesis worked to American democracy's advantage.

CHAPTER SIX

CHRISTIANITY AND AMERICA'S POLITICAL HEALTH

Freedom sees religion as the companion of its struggles and triumphs, the cradle of its infancy, and the divine source of its rights. Religion is considered as the guardian of mores, and mores are regarded as the guarantee of the laws and pledge for the maintenance of freedom itself (47).

Tocqueville's discussion of American Christianity's political usefulness has two levels, each with a different purpose. At some points in the *Democracy*, he presents Christianity as the most important of America's political institutions, providing support for the birth and growth of her political freedom and shaping the mores essential for her survival. His goal here was to strengthen a tottering French Church by showing skeptical liberals that Christianity, when properly reformed, is not an enemy, but an ally of freedom. I shall discuss this part of Tocqueville's analysis in the present chapter as well as his account of the threats that extreme quality poses to freedom. An understanding of these threats will highlight his depiction of Christianity's positive political role.

At other points in the book, however, Tocqueville gives a more nuanced account of American Christianity's contribution to freedom which reveals what it failed to do for this cause. His aim here was to warn liberal statesmen convinced of religion's political utility against relying too heavily on it as democracy matures. I shall consider this account in chapter 7. In Tocqueville's final judgment, America in the 1830s was less politically healthy than it seemed. He considered the quality of American statesmanship dismal, for example, and the twin evils of slavery and race prejudice a national disgrace. Tocqueville shows that Christianity did little to ameliorate these conditions. He further shows that even the healthy elements of America's character were shaped less by piety than by secular ethical principles. The upshot of all this is that Tocqueville considered Christianity a political asset in the 1830s, but one of limited value.

CHRISTIANITY AS THE SOURCE OF AMERICAN POLITICAL PRINCIPLES

American political life, as Tocqueville described it, was based on a notion of justice, or "idea of rights," which defined the scope of freedom and distinguished legitimate government from tyranny (238). This idea originated in the Christian spirit of freedom or, more specifically, in the doctrine that all human beings had an "equal right . . . at birth to liberty" (439).[1] Christ introduced this principle into the world to initiate the democratic revolution and to give his imprimatur to freedom. During the course of its historical development, it eventually transformed all aspects of life in the Christian West including its social condition and politics, its economics and intimate relationships, and finally, the shape of its religion itself. Christian ethics,

Tocqueville wrote, are "the great source of modern morality" (Tocqueville 1959, 208; Tocqueville 1951–, 9:59).

The first accomplishment of the principle of equal freedom was to lift the hopes of human beings rather than to liberate them (446). The Christian religion was born in the Roman Empire, where a large part of humanity lived under the sovereignty of the Caesars. Although there were differences among the various peoples subject to Rome, all were so weak and insignificant with respect to the emperor that their status relative to each other was one of slavish equality (46).

After the fall of the Empire, the Roman world split into its component parts, and medieval society was born. The powerful of each nation united against the weak and subdued them by force. The victors formed military aristocracies bent on perpetuating their rule, and the defeated became agricultural slaves who toiled on the conquered land. The basic principles of medieval society were hereditary servitude and inequality. Although these principles were fundamentally opposed to the Christian idea of rights, the Church supported the aristocracy for the sake of the faith and lent itself "as far as it could, to the new tendencies which came into existence as humanity was broken up" (446).

Although medieval Christianity seemed to forsake the principle of equal freedom, it never did so entirely. The Church made the principle politically potent by allowing all men freely to enter its ranks. When the clergy acquired political power, it introduced social mobility into government, and he "who would have vegetated as a serf in eternal servitude could, as a priest, take his place among the nobles and often take precedence over kings" (10). The Church's acquisition of political power, therefore, marked the beginning of the process which eventually made equality the dominant force in Christian political life (16).

Martin Luther inaugurated another distinct stage in this process when he directly and explicitly introduced the principle of equal freedom into the religious realm.[2] Luther used this principle to democratize Christianity's ecclesiastical structure by eliminating the Catholic hierarchy among believers. In Protestant churches all members were equal and clergymen were chosen democratically rather than ordained or consecrated from above. This principle also overturned the Church's monopoly on Scriptural interpretation and subjected some religious dogmas to the scrutiny of private judgment, as we have seen.

Tocqueville considered these democratic changes important milestones in Western political history. Although Luther's primary theological goal was to rescue Christian orthodoxy from the corruptions of Catholicism, his reforms produced a rippling effect which fragmented the Christian world and drove the Puritans to America (430–431).

When the Puritans emigrated to the New World, Old Testament-based theories of divine right still governed European political life. Absolute monarchs ruled most European countries and political participation was more limited than it had been during the Middle Ages (45, 431). The Puritans broke decisively with their contemporaries by establishing the first modern, free democracies (18, 33–34, 39, 45–46). A variety of factors contributed to this accomplishment including their high level of social and economic equality, their experiences in British politics, their religious innovations, the harshness of their soil, and the almost complete absence of slavery (33, 344, n. 34).

The most important factor, however, was their innovative politics. Tocqueville considered the New England Puritans applied political theorists as well as religious reformers, and credited them with a highly sophisticated understanding of law, government, and the "principles of true liberty" (33). Armed with this knowledge, they extended the spirit of freedom into the political realm, a world until then governed by obedience to religious authority. This move allowed them to put the "boldest speculations of humanity" into practice. "Under their manipulation," Tocqueville writes,

> Political principles, laws, and human institutions seem malleable things which can at will be adapted and combined. The barriers which hemmed in the society in which they were brought up fall before them; old views which have ruled the world for centuries vanish; almost limitless opportunities lie open in a world without horizon; the spirit of man rushes forward to explore it in every direction (47).

The Puritans were America's founders, in Tocqueville's view, because their new political ideas formed the basis of American constitutionalism and of our democratic political culture (33, 35). Tocqueville knew, of course, that Virginia was the first American colony, established thirteen years before the Pilgrims landed on Plymouth Rock. In contrast to the Puritans who came to the New World for principled reasons, however, the first Virginians were generally ne'er do wells motivated by the desire for gain (34–35). Indeed, by introducing slavery to America, they grievously harmed the cause of freedom and gave the South its distinctive, aristocratic character (348–349, 375–376). Tocqueville believed that Southern laws and mores were fundamentally unjust and doomed to perish at the hands of the more democratic New England principles (363, 399–400, 704).

The chief Puritan contribution to American political life was a doctrine of popular sovereignty, based on a robust concept of political freedom. The Mayflower Compact and other like convenants established the right of free and equal individuals under God to form a "civil body politic" and made consent the *de facto* basis for political authority (38–39, n. 11). Local independence, which Tocqueville considered the "mainspring and life-blood of American freedom," was widely established in New England by 1650 (44). Puritan governments were highly democratic empowering all citizens to participate directly in public affairs. Although Puritan townships were legally under Great Britain's jurisdiction, they operated, for all practical purposes, as independent republics. They made their own laws, levied their own taxes, controlled their internal affairs, and held their magistrates accountable (43, 44).

As the doctrine of popular sovereignty gradually spread to most of the English colonies, it shaped American mores embedding the Christian idea of rights deep within the American character (58–59, 63). After the revolution, this doctrine emerged from the townships to underpin all the state governments. According to Tocqueville, this fact determined the essential nature of the U.S. Constitution. In his view, the basic principles of our national government were "spread throughout society before its time, existed independently of it, and only had to be modified" to call it to life (59, 61).[3]

Tocqueville did not mean to disparage Thomas Jefferson or the Framers of the Constitution by subordinating them to the Puritans. Although he considered equal freedom well established by 1776 and ignores the Declaration of Independence in the *Democracy,* he called Jefferson "the most powerful apostle of democracy there has ever been" as we have seen (261). Also, he considered the Framers as a group remarkable for their enlightenment, patriotism, candor, foresight, and love of freedom. In fact, he believed that the leading Framers, such as George Washington and James Madison, were "the men of greatest intelligence and noblest character ever to have appeared in the New World" (114). His judgments on these three Virginians qualify to a certain extent his admiration for New England and his criticism of Southern aristocracy.

Tocqueville also admired the Constitution and discussed it extensively in the *Democracy*. He especially liked the principles of judicial review, indirect election, and other constitutional restraints on the power of the majority (103–104, 153, 201, 697–699). In general, though, he considered the Constitution more a by-product than a source of democratic sovereignty and its new national government less important to freedom than a strong tradition of local self-government (Kraynak 1987, 1187, 1189). Further, he believed that the Constitution worked largely because the Puritans made a critical mass of Americans self-governing, public spirited citizens before the document was written. The same frame of government resting on a weaker national character, he argued, would be much less likely to accomplish its goals (307).

THE TYRANNY OF THE MAJORITY

The Constitution's greatest accomplishment, in Tocqueville's view, was to nationalize the Christian idea of rights. He considered this idea rationally as well as religiously just because it satisfied the "universal and permanent" needs of mankind as we know them without divine revelation (616). These needs include a measure of physical well-being and an opportunity for moral and intellectual growth. Tocqueville was well aware that American democracy, like all democracies, gave short shrift to the interests of the few and this concerned him. Yet his respect for America's economic and political achievements and his belief that democracy was more just than aristocracy made him a firm, although somewhat melancholy, democrat (49, 231–235, 704).

Tocqueville's admiration for American democracy was qualified, however by a keen awareness of its short-comings. His analysis of these flaws is justly famous, and an essential part of his "new political science." Ironically, he considered equality itself a highly prob-lematic principle. Tocqueville believed that democratic political life comports with freedom ideally and up to a point. But he considered them separate and different entities capable of clashing under certain circumstances (503–504, 667–668). Unrestrained economic freedom, for example, can lead to vast political inequalities (555–558). Likewise, political equality diminishes freedom when pushed beyond its natural and just limits. De-mocracy is especially prone to this latter danger be-cause the people love liberty lukewarmly, but worship equality passionately (504–506). As Tocqueville put it in a famous statement:

> There is indeed a manly and legitimate passion for
> equality which rouses in all men a desire to be strong
> and respected. This passion tends to elevate the little
> man to the rank of the great. But the human heart also
> nourishes a debased taste for equality, which leads the
> weak to want to drag the strong down to their level and
> which induces men to prefer equality in servitude to
> inequality in freedom (57).

Tocqueville believed that the "tyranny of the majority" was the most direct and immediate threat to America's political health arising from excessive equality. He first shows, in describing this particular evil, that the term popular government is a misnomer. In fact, the major-ity, not the people, rule in the United States, a distinc-tion democrats tend to forget (246, 58, 379). While the majority governs in the people's name, it often pursues its own good at the expense of dissenting or powerless minorities (250–253). This danger is exacerbated by the majority's tendency to misperceive the public interest, to consider its willfulness just and reasonable, and to engage in excessive lawmaking.

Majority tyranny appeared early in American history as Puritan lawgivers "constantly invaded the sphere of conscience" in ways large and small. Most significantly, they forgot "the great principle of religious liberty which they themselves claimed in Europe," enforcing "attendance at divine service" and severely punishing Christians "who chose to worship God with a ritual other than their own" (42–43).

In the 1830s, despotic majorities were firmly in control of America's state governments (260n). In most of these, legislatures were all-powerful, thereby inflating the majority's natural strength. The people tightly controlled these legislatures by choosing their representatives frequently and, in most cases, directly. Furthermore, state executives and judges generally pandered to lawmakers. Thus, while state governments were representative in theory, majorities governed almost directly at the expense of the wealthy, of the intellectually gifted, and of powerless minorities, such as the hapless blacks (153–154, 241, 246–247, 250–256).[4]

THE WEAKENING OF NATIONAL CHARACTER: MEN

Tocqueville thought that, in the long run, excessive equality weakens rather than strengthens the popular disposition to govern, and that future American majorities would more likely be passive than overly energetic. This passivity would result, he feared, from certain traits of character fostered by democracy as it matures.

The first of these is individualism, a pernicious feeling which draws democratic men away from society and causes them to devote their energy solely to personal matters. In traditional European aristocracies, a hierarchical class structure bound all people together by firm and lasting social and political ties. All classes, from the highest to the lowest, depended on each other for certain necessities in ways that bred a mutual sense of obligation. These ties existed to a certain extent among the New England Puritans whose sense of religious duty included love and concern for others. As democracy eliminated class-based distinctions and weakened religious fervor, it severed the bonds which held people together. Large numbers of men became economically independent and as a result erroneously believed they controlled their own destinies. This false sense of independence transformed traditional feelings of obligation into radical self-interest (506–508).

Such was the case during the course of American history. New England's soil was inhospitable to a territorial aristocracy (33–34) and the abolition of primogeniture during the revolutionary era broke up the occasional landed estate, and with it the extended families essential to a class-based society. This led many of America's elite to sell their inheritance, enter the business or professional world, and join the working masses in pursuing private gain (51–54). A general decline in the binding power of religious obligation accompanied these changes. By the 1830s, virtually all Americans were self-centered, self-reliant, gainfully employed, and highly mobile (508, 536, 550).

Tocqueville's Americans, like most democrats, also worshipped physical at the expense of spiritual well-being (530, 639). In part, their material preoccupations derived from democracy's atomism and fluid class structure. In traditional aristocracies, economic status was fixed from birth. The rich and poor took their respective lots in life for granted and detached themselves somewhat from economic concerns (507–508). The democratic and more economically equal American Puritans did so as well, though to a much lesser extent (47).

In Jacksonian America, however, natural abundance, social mobility, and a decline in piety encouraged economic aspirations and a work-for-profit oriented mentality. Since the marketplace was generally competitive and capricious, economic uncertainty haunted the nation's imagination making men restless and sad despite their relative wealth. Their ill-chosen remedies for these ailments were comfort, convenience, and more wealth (530, 535–537, 639).

THE WEAKENING OF NATIONAL CHARACTER: WOMEN

Tocqueville feared that excessive egalitarianism would also adversely affect American women and his short discussion of them in the *Democracy* is highly significant. The reason for this is clear. Tocqueville believed that women shape mores and, as we have seen, that good mores are essential to a country's political health. Thus, he considered everything bearing on "the status of women, their habits, and their thoughts" to be of "great political importance" (590).[5]

Tocqueville's discussion of women emphasizes how democracy affects their sexual behavior and especially their propensity to license. He believed that widespread sexual license seriously threatens political freedom. In his view, unbridled sensuality exalts selfishness and private pleasure, distorts judgment and sensibility, and destabilizes personal relationships. After disrupting family life, it inevitably exacts a large political toll (291). Such was the case in France where a high incidence of unstable marriages and illicit affairs undermined political authority and weakened public spiritedness (599).

Although he never explains why he holds women responsible for society's sexual morality, we may assume
he followed Rousseau in stressing their ability to control the sexual approaches of men and to establish the
legitimacy of children (Rousseau 1979, 359–361).

Tocqueville first argues that women are only licentious when forced to marry against their will (595–597).
This frequently occurred in nineteenth-century France
where the aristocratic custom of arranged marriage survived the democratic deluge (595–596; Tocqueville 1955,
83). America reduced that danger, he suggests, by re-
specting the right of women to choose their own marriage partners. Under these circumstances, "no girl . . .
feels that she cannot become the wife of the man who
likes her best," Tocqueville notes, "and that makes ir-
regular morals before marriage very difficult" (595). The
same cause indirectly promotes marital fidelity by making public opinion highly intolerant of adultery (596).

On a deeper level, though, Tocqueville shows that,
even in America, unchecked equality can lead to license. There are several reasons for this. Tocqueville
believed that the sexual passions are the "most tyrannical passions of the human heart" and thus extremely
difficult to control (591). Americans liberated these passions to a certain extent by granting women great freedom during their youth, a time when people are most
impatient, their passions most unstable, and their tastes
most unformed (590–592). At the same time, American
moralists made physical attraction a natural and legitimate basis for marriage (595–597). This combination of
factors could not help but increase the intensity of desire. "Every passion grows stronger the more attention
it gets," he warned, "and is swollen by every effort to
satisfy it" (552n).

Tocqueville also believed that excessive equality
threatened the democratic family by undermining its

traditional division of labor and its traditional principle of authority, namely rule by the male. Such was the wish of some Europeans who carried sexual equality to what he considered an absurd extreme. "Confusing the divergent attributes of the sexes," he wrote, they "claim to make of man and woman creatures who are, not equal only, but actually similar. They would attribute the same functions to both, impose the same duties, and grant the same rights; they would have them share everything—work, pleasure, public affairs" (600–601). Tocqueville considered this sort of equality, which is highly popular today, unnatural, degrading to both sexes, and a chief cause of adultery, the form of license most harmful to the family and hence to society as a whole (592, 601).

DEMOCRATIC DESPOTISM

Tocqueville considered France more likely than America to succumb to one man rule or the rule of the few. Yet he suggests that selfish materialism and apathy could someday make Americans vulnerable to tyranny, especially if this dangerous mix outpaces their education, their political experience, and their tolerance for instability (540–541, 671, 690). Usurpers need not "drag their rights away from citizens of this type," Tocqueville warns. Such citizens will "voluntarily let them go" in exchange for prosperity and "good order" (540). Ironically, tyranny generally impoverishes its victims, and those who buy fortune with freedom eventually lose both (539–541).

Tocqueville thought it more likely, however, that America would forfeit the essence of political freedom while keeping its outward form. Democracies naturally centralize political power, he argued, by undermining the secondary bodies which defend private rights and particular interests. America was not immune from this tendency, though blessed with a multilayered division of political authority. Tocqueville believed that the sectional crisis caused by slavery endangered the Union as he knew it. He thought, however, that if the South ever became firmly attached to the Union, the national government could consolidate its authority at the expense of the states and localities and in the end establish what he called an "administrative" or "democratic" despotism (382, 688–670, 693; Hancock 1992, 133–135).[6]

Tocqueville's description of democratic despotism is one of the most haunting parts of the *Democracy*. While the people may choose their rulers in this regime, they generally refrain from all other types of political activity. Considering the government their own, they allow it to extend its power indefinitely as long as it treats them equally and promotes their economic well-being. The more dependent the people become on their government, the more willing they are to sacrifice their rights to its political designs. The rulers, in return, guide and instruct them in the various incidents of life. Eventually, the people lose the faculties of thinking, feeling, and acting for themselves and come to resemble a flock of "timid and hardworking animals with the government as its shepherd" (692, 694).[7]

CHRISTIANITY AND THE MAINTENANCE OF FREEDOM

Tocqueville suggests that the Christian spirit of religion protected Jacksonian America against both the worst forms of majority tyranny and the character disorders which cause democratic despotism over time. American Christianity taught that God intended rights to be used for moral and religious purposes and would punish those who misuse them or violate the rights of others (289–290, 292).[8] John Winthrop's definition of freedom (which Tocqueville cites approvingly as "liberty for that only which is just and good") captures this limiting function quite well (46).

These religious ideas enhanced public morality, making American majorities at least somewhat sensitive to minority rights. They also fostered political stability in a democratic milieu where the clash of interests, ambitions, and parties constantly threatened to upset the status quo. Finally, they established "insurmountable barriers" to the schemes of the politically ambitious, forcing them to respect rights in both word and deed (292). During the early period of America's national history, these barriers moderated the behavior of America's more dangerous political characters. "Up till now," Tocqueville notes, "no one in the United States has dared to profess the maxim that everything is allowed in the interests of society" (292, 312).

American Christianity also bolstered private morality against excessive egalitarianism in a number of indirect ways. Tocqueville considered this form of support for freedom even more valuable than its direct, public support. In fact, it was "just when it is not speaking of freedom at all," he concluded, that religion "best teaches the Americans the art of being free" (290).

On the most intimate level, Christianity strengthened America's national character by regulating the private behavior of women. The following passage of the *Democracy* indicates the importance Tocqueville attributes to this role:

> I do not doubt for an instant that the great severity of mores which one notices in the United States has its primary origin in beliefs. There religion . . . reigns supreme in the souls of the women, and it is women who shape mores. Certainly of all the countries in the world

America is the one in which the marriage tie is most respected and where the highest and truest conception of conjugal happiness has been conceived (291).

Tocqueville clearly suggests here that religion's continuing influence on women was responsible for America's high level of sexual morality (see also 32). Traditional Christianity's sexual code required virginity outside of marriage, continence and fidelity within marriage, and the strict avoidance of all forms of license (41–43). He also suggests that America's "conception of conjugal happiness" was Christian in nature, that is based on the marital principles of the Bible. These principles, as Americans interpreted them, accorded both sexes equal freedom and dignity, but required them to play different roles in life. American men in the 1830s generally ruled the household, managed the family's external relations, and earned its daily bread. American women were responsible for domestic management, rearing the children, and the overall morals of the family. Although these principles fell far short of the full equality advocated by European radicals of the time, they were, in Tocqueville's view, generally considered just by Americans of both sexes (600–603).

As Tocqueville describes it, Christian piety gave American married life a moral seriousness which sharply curtailed the external freedom women enjoyed when single. Public opinion confined American wives to the "quiet sphere of domestic duties" and forced them to submit to even "stricter obligations" than their European counterparts (601, 592). Indeed, Tocqueville suggests that a woman's contact with male society virtually ended on her wedding day (but see p. 243). Although moralists defended these restrictions on a variety of grounds, their central purpose was to establish the "regularity" of a married woman's life, or, in other words, to insure that she remain chaste. These new shackles testify to the gravity with which Americans regarded female adultery. In their view, no other crime posed such a grave threat to family stability and to the country's moral fiber (592).

Today's readers might well view Tocqueville's claim that such women were genuinely free with a certain skepticism, if not disbelief. The hardness of their lives and the constraints they suffered elicit both our sympathy and indignation (731–733). From Tocqueville's perspective, however, American marriage constituted a revolutionary advance in the relations between the sexes. The reason is fairly straightforward. Despite their various disabilities, married American women occupied a higher station in life than any of their European counterparts (603). Although European men flattered and pampered their wives, they ruled them despotically on the basis of a grossly exaggerated sense of male superiority. Women could only exert significant influence over their husbands through the arbitrary use of their sexual power (602).

In contrast, American wives enjoyed an unprecedented equality with their spouses. They entered marriage via a contract which assumed both partners to be free and morally responsible adults (596). Their submission to conjugal authority was based on consent rather than coercion and limited by the respect generally accorded their judgment and virtue (601–602). Also, the duties of American women were considered equal, if not superior, in dignity to those of their husbands. The most important of these were transmitting the country's Christian heritage to future generations and nourishing their love of freedom (291, 590). Tocqueville thought that American wives were more adept at these tasks than their husbands, despite their selfish propensities. This was due partly to their greater natural piety, and partly to the shield their confinement provided against economic individualism.

Tocqueville believed that America's decision to grant women a significant role in transmitting Christian mores was a stroke of political genius. In aristocracies, men were considered the arbiters of mores, thus violating what he considered nature's intention (587). This perversion denied women the opportunity to use their talents constructively and reinforced both domestic and political tyranny. American wives occupied an exalted station, on the other hand, largely because their moral pedagogy effectively complemented their chastity in serving the cause of political freedom. Indeed, by stressing the paramount importance of mores, Tocqueville suggests that women contributed more than men to America's freedom despite their lack of formal political power (590, 600–603).

The high regard in which Americans held their wives and daughters also led them to take strict measures against external threats to their virtue. They were more solicitous of women than the French, who treated female vulnerability with considerable contempt (602–603). In the United States, public opinion tolerated neither language nor literature which a Christian woman would find offensive. While there was no official censorship as in France, no American author was even tempted to write licentious books, or for that matter, books hostile to Christianity (256). Americans also rejected the French double standard for adultery. With them, Tocqueville noted "the seducer is as much dishonored as his victim" (602). Finally, while the French treated rapists with a certain tolerance, Americans considered their crime a capital offense. The United States was so safe in the 1830s that young women could "set out on a long journey alone and without fear" (603).

American Christianity also fostered the growth of voluntary associations which checked excessive individualism by drawing people out of the private sphere.

Religious freedom led to the rise of an "innumerable multitude of sects" all committed to freedom and powerful in its defense (290, 516). While differing on theological grounds, they all agreed on "the duties of men to one another" and promoted the performance of these duties in their work (290). Their moral call to action, strengthened by public opinion, also caused Americans to join other associations devoted to Christian purposes. In the 1830s, these included seminaries, missionary groups, hospitals, prison reform organizations, and temperance societies (513–516).

Finally, Christianity elevated American tastes. Democrats, as we have seen, tend to become so wholly obsessed with physical well-being that they lose their love for freedom and their ability to defend it. Christianity counters these tendencies by purifying, controlling, and restraining materialism (448). Christian precepts regarding Sabbath observance were particularly helpful in this regard, requiring people to devote at least some time to spiritual concerns. In America, both law and public opinion rigorously enforced these precepts, proscribing all work and, in most cases, all frivolous leisure (542; Tocqueville 1985, 48).

While workaday America of the 1830s was a place of unrelieved business and bustle, Sunday was intensely quite. On this day, trade and industry stopped, stores were deserted, and every family went to church and then studied the Bible at home. Thus, for at least one day a week, Tocqueville noted, Americans entered an "ideal world where all is great, pure, and eternal," and the "soul comes into its own" (542; see 712–714).

Tocqueville considered this enforced preoccupation with the soul the greatest political advantage Americans derived from their religious beliefs. Christianity, like most religions, teaches that the soul is both immaterial and immortal (544). These ideas, linked to a conception of divine reward and punishment, provided a powerful incentive for moral virtue. Concern for the soul also gave people a certain respect for, if not desire for, a spiritually-oriented life (542). Finally, Christianity gave Americans an otherworldly motive for the sacrifices of life and property that every political community occasionally requires. "It will always be difficult to make a man live well," Tocqueville remarked, "if he will not face death" (528).

Tocqueville admired Christianity above all other religions, deeming it the only faith truly suitable for promoting democratic freedom. Yet he was willing to countenance any religion that fostered belief in the soul's immortality because he valued this belief so highly. This tolerance extended even to the doctrine of metapsychosis which teaches that the soul passes into the body of an animal or some other creature after death (544). Despite the spiritual shortcomings of this doctrine, Tocqueville concluded, it makes people "consider the body as the secondary and inferior part of [their] nature," and thereby deserves a certain measure of support (544–545).

Finally, while Tocqueville doesn't stress this, he shows that Christian spirituality served America's material as well as her moral needs. "Whatever elevates, enlarges, and expands the soul makes it more able to succeed even in those undertakings which are not the soul's concern," he noted (546–547). Tocqueville admired America's economic prosperity despite his fears regarding her excessive materialism. In a strange twist to his argument, he shows that the same otherworldly doctrines which justified poverty in medieval times bolstered America's economic strength. By teaching Americans how to resist their immediate, selfish passions for the sake of eternity, Christianity fostered the patience, tenacity, and foresight which made them so successful in managing their temporal affairs (528–530).

CONCLUSION

A brief summary of this chapter is now in order. Tocqueville portrayed American Christianity's political role in a most positive light, at least on one level of his argument. His New England Puritans brought the Christian idea of rights to America in the early seventeenth century and transformed it into a robust concept of political freedom. Here it developed over the next two centuries, forming the basis for American constitutionalism under Christianity's moral guidance, but in opposition to its traditional political claims. During the early republic Christianity was the "first" of America's political institutions. While its spirit of freedom gave political freedom a religious basis, its spirit of religion checked the majority's tyrannical tendencies as it strengthened its healthy political impulses against the degrading effects of extreme equality.

CHAPTER SEVEN

THE SECULARIZATION OF AMERICAN MORALS

Do you not see that religions are growing weak and that the conception of the sanctity of rights is vanishing? Do you not see that mores are changing and that the moral conception of rights is being obliterated with them? . . . If amid this universal collapse you do not succeed in linking the idea of rights to personal interest, which provides the only stable point in the human heart, what other means will be left to you to govern the world if not fear? (239)

So far, Tocqueville's Americans appear to be a deeply religious people with morals ultimately shaped by the Bible. This impression, which strongly supports Tocqueville's claim that faith is essential to freedom, is highly misleading. In the end, he considered "self-interest properly understood," or enlightened self-love, the primary source for American morals in the 1830s. This principle was a byproduct of the same spirit of freedom which by then had secularized American religion and politics. It presupposes rational individuals whose right to make final moral judgments is as absolute as their right to determine religious and political truth.

129

In this chapter, I shall first explain how self-interest properly understood supplanted the Puritans' theologically-oriented moral principles. I shall then examine how enlightened self-love shaped two components of American morality which Tocqueville initially presents as being solidly grounded in Christianity—chastity and the idea of rights. Finally, I shall consider Tocqueville's assessment of this principle's moral efficacy. Although he admired self-interest properly understood, he thought it wholly inadequate to deal with the country's grievous racial problem. This judgment seriously qualifies his initial optimistic appraisal of America's moral resources.

FROM RELIGIOUS TO SECULAR MORALITY

As we have seen, New England Puritan morality was based on the spirit of religion, Tocqueville's term for a cluster of principles linked to biblical orthodoxy. First among these was a lively sense of human sinfulness, traceable to the human tendency to abuse God-given freedom. This was the "*liberty* of corrupt nature" which John Winthrop referred to in a speech quoted by Tocqueville as the liberty of "*men* and *beasts* to do what they list" (46).

The Puritans, as is well known, were especially concerned with rooting out sexual license. Their remedy for this and other forms of private vice, aside from prayer, was to require strict obedience to a comprehensive state-enforced penal code drawn from the Pentateuch. Scriptural legalism was so pervasive in Puritan New England that "hardly a sin" was "not subject to the magistrate's censure" (42). The Puritans punished rape, adultery, and incest by death (along with blasphemy and sorcery), harshly repressed intercourse between unmarried persons, and fined and reprimanded those guilty of kissing in public and other minor indiscretions (41–43).

Puritan public morality was also based on a sense of duty, or on the Christian premise that (in Tocqueville's words) "we must do good to our fellows for love of God" (529). This precept led the Puritans to love and to serve their communities disinterestedly. They considered wealth instrumental to piety and taxed themselves to provide for a multitude of social needs generally ignored by other societies of the time. These included relief for the poor, public works, and an extensive system of public education (44, 45). Although the Puritans tolerated material prosperity, their concern for wealth did not significantly diminish their piety. "If any man among us make religion as twelve and the world as thirteen," warned a Puritan divine cited by Tocqueville, "such a one hath not the spirit of a true New-Englandman" (720). The use of wealth or any worldly good for selfish ends was considered a perverse form of idolatry, "the grand enemy of *truth* and *peace*" (46).

Tocqueville's claim at several points in the *Democracy* that such ideas governed American morals in the nineteenth as well as the seventeenth century is not conclusive. He shows in fact that a trend toward greater moral autonomy accompanied the growth of political freedom and religious individualism as American democracy matured. By the 1830s, private interest had become the "chief if not the only driving force behind all behavior," making Tocqueville's Americans more acquisitive, more preoccupied with comfort and convenience, and more self-reliant than traditional Christians were entitled to be (527). These Americans also came to believe that reason rather than revelation was the "source of moral authority," and that each individual had the right to pursue happiness according to his or her own lights (374). Such views rendered them unwilling to accept or conform to a biblically oriented moral code.

Although Tocqueville's Americans considered themselves morally autonomous, their moral freedom was, in fact, as illusory as their religious freedom. Free moral agents are rare, he believed, and most people when given the choice will surrender their freedom to some external authority (434). In democracy, this authority is public opinion, which imposes its moral as well as its intellectual will on individuals by "some mighty pressure of the mind" (435). The majority's perceived needs and beliefs determine the content of democratic morality which may or may not coincide with Christian principles (435–436).

Thus, the majority supplied Tocqueville's Americans with a quantity of "ready-made" moral opinions which relieved them of "the necessity of forming [their] own" (435). Although American public opinion in the 1830s had a strong Christian component, its dominant strains were secular. These included a faith in reason, a preference for material over spiritual goods, a belief in freedom as an ultimate end, and, above all, an emphasis on the individual. Americans held these principles with an unChristian pride that Tocqueville both admired and disdained. In contrast to the Puritans who were humble at least before God, they had "an immensely high opinion of themselves" and were "not far from believing that they form a species apart from the rest of the human race" (374). This smug sense of superiority bore little resemblance to the Puritans' view of themselves as God's chosen people (see 37).

These developments paved the way for the triumph of self-interest properly understood. This principle's basic premise is that "self-love" if "enlightened" will produce "just" and "honest" behavior (374, 526). Under its influence, for example, one respects the property of others not because theft is sinful, but because such respect will secure one's own possessions (238). Americans, rich and poor, found such notions easy to learn, easy to follow, and "wonderfully agreeable" to their weaknesses (526–527). In fact, their belief in the doctrine's explanatory power led them to discount their real natural sympathies and selfless impulses. "Americans are hardly prepared to admit that they do give way to emotions of this sort," Tocqueville remarked. "They prefer to give credit to their philosophy rather than to themselves" (526).

SEXUAL MORALITY REVISITED

Tocqueville's extended discussion of sexual morality in Volume II of the *Democracy* shows how powerful he believed this new moral theory actually was. As we have seen, Tocqueville initially attributed America's high level of chastity to the influence of Christianity on the mores of American women. He shows later, however, that by the 1830s, chastity's religious "safeguards" had been largely replaced by a moral education based on freedom and enlightened self-love (591). Tocqueville's account of this education doesn't mention interest explicitly, perhaps because he wished to avoid offending the pious. Yet a careful reading of his analysis reveals its pervasive presence.

During the 1830s, American moralists instilled the principle of enlightened self-love into the souls of American women through an elaborate system of education. Traditional Christianity generally regarded women as "seductive but incomplete beings," whose sexual frailties required severe restrictions on their freedom (602). In Tocqueville's France, for example, where the Church still governed the young, girls received a "timid, withdrawn, almost cloistered" upbringing aimed at keeping them ignorant of the world and repressing their sexual desires (591). This training reinforced the patriarchal structure of French society and created adult women who were fearful, dependent, and self-deprecating (602).

Tocqueville's Americans relied on freedom rather than authority to educate their women. Although he first links this use of freedom to America's Protestant heritage, he later shows that it signifies a virtual break with religious tradition (590). While everything Puritan women learned about sexual conduct was "classified, coordinated, foreseen, and decided in advance" (47), their American descendants were taught to make independent moral judgments based on a rational view of the world (374, 590–592). The source of this new orientation was not the Christian spirit of religion, but the philosophical method adopted by Americans as the Christian spirit of freedom became secularized (429–433).

American moralists hoped that a free view of the world would convince young women of the advantages of being chaste. They clearly recognized that the virtue of their charges would often be in danger and that "incredible efforts" were required for them to attain self-mastery (591). Part of their pedagogy consisted of training women to understand the value of chastity as well as the nature of eros. They also taught the young how to preserve their virtue through a combination of will power, self-confidence, and wit. These lessons, of course, required women to learn a considerable amount about men through mixing in society. On the whole, their sophisticated knowledge of human nature "surprised and almost frightened" Tocqueville (591). American moralists turned to religion for aid only when all else failed. Yet even their anguished appeals to piety were most likely variations on the theme of enlightened self-love (528–530, 591–592).

At first glance, it is difficult to understand why American women considered it so advantageous to be chaste. Indeed, given the temptations they experienced and the general weakness of traditional authority, their self-restraint was quite remarkable. Tocqueville resolves this paradox by showing that the sexual freedom the young enjoyed was more apparent than real. In the 1830s, American public opinion condemned license with unparalleled severity making sexual misconduct a highly risky business (595, 622).

Tocqueville attributed part of this harshness to the influence of Christianity which, even in its weakened condition, continued to shape public thinking to a considerable extent (592). Its chief cause, however, was the pervasive hunger for material gain engendered by equality. During Tocqueville's time, America was a trading and industrial community devoted almost exclusively to exploiting the country's vast natural resources. Americans honored chastity most because it fostered commercial habits, kept families productive, and helped maintain the political stability essential to prosperity (621–622). Tocqueville stresses the importance of these factors in order to emphasize the extent of American chastity's secular support. Even the survival of Christianity, as we have seen, was partly due to its accommodations to the national love of wealth. Chastity's status in American religion would be far less secure, he implies, if it hindered rather than served economic growth (447–448).

The connection Tocqueville draws between chastity and public opinion sheds new light on the freedom enjoyed by American women. Put simply, it was not intended to allow the married or the unmarried significant moral choices in sexual matters, but rather to show all women that chastity was essential to their future happiness. What an apt student quickly learned from her exposure to the world was the very high cost of sexual misbehavior. She could not "for a moment depart from the usages accepted by her contemporaries without immediately putting in danger her peace of mind, her reputation, and her very social existence" (593). Tocqueville was well aware that pressure of this sort made women chaste in conduct rather than disposition and therefore less than truly virtuous (Tocqueville 1960, 114). He believed, however, that this type of female virtue was all that could be generally hoped for in democratic times (590–592).

This connection also sheds light on the sexual behavior of American men, a subject Tocqueville does not discuss extensively. Democracy made our forefathers exceedingly practical, preoccupied with acquiring wealth, and unerotic (598, 532–534). Taught by the doctrine of enlightened self-love that asceticism was necessary to the attainment of long-range economic goals (528–529), they generally sought domestic tranquility and shunned romantic adventures of any kind (598). (Tocqueville found no rakes of the type that existed in France in America [Tocqueville 1985, 40]). Their docility was also due partly to marital freedom and to the tight constraints of public opinion.

American men did have a weakness for visiting prostitutes, a vice which required little time, emotional involvement, or imagination. Lawgivers tolerated prostitution because it helped prevent adultery and thus, in an indirect way, kept national morality sound. Tocqueville considered this policy a regrettable but wise concession to the intractability of male lust (598; Tocqueville 1960, 223).

THE NEW IDEA OF RIGHTS

Perhaps the most fundamental change in American moral life since Puritan times concerned the prevailing idea of rights. Tocqueville, as we have seen, considered this idea, or the "conception of virtue applied to the world of politics," the critical factor in determining a country's potential for greatness (237, 238). The Puritan idea of rights was Christian in origin, scope, and purpose. It held that Christ introduced equal freedom into the world for providential reasons and that it exists only for the sake of doing just and good deeds.

In a key statement regarding America's national character in the 1830s, Tocqueville reveals why this idea of rights was no longer viable:

> Do you not see that religions are growing weak and that the conception of the sanctity of rights is vanishing? Do you not see that mores are changing and that the moral conception of rights is being obliterated with them?
>
> Do you not notice how on all sides beliefs are giving way to arguments, and feelings to calculations? If amid this universal collapse you do not succeed in linking the idea of rights to personal interest, which provides the only stable point in the human heart, what other means will be left to you to govern the world, if not fear (239)?

By the 1830s, Tocqueville's Americans valued their political rights less for their religious significance than because they enjoyed them. While they were generally as patriotic, law-abiding, and politically active as the Puritans, their public spiritedness derived from the link they perceived between their country's well-being and their own, rather than from a genuine concern for the common good (235–237). The doctrine of self-interest properly understood was also the moving force behind public service. Aspiring politicians viewed holding office as a lucrative career and helping their constituents as the best way to gain and retain popular support (220, 510).

Tocqueville illustrates the political changes wrought by the new concept of rights in his description of the New England township, the direct descendant of the

Puritan community. Although the spirit of freedom governed New England political life during the 1830s as it did during Puritan times, the level of religiosity in this area of the country had declined significantly. While the Puritans established a limited degree of separation between church and state, their governments, as we have seen, were responsible for enforcing orthodoxy and Christian mores (41, 43). Tocqueville's New Englanders allowed their governments no more authority over their behavior than necessary to secure their private, secular interests (66). Although traces of Puritanism existed in many local laws, mores were significantly relaxed (although by no means loose), and politically sponsored religious persecution was virtually non-existent (712). In strictly religious matters, the townspeople of Tocqueville's New England held themselves accountable to God alone. Instead of using their freedom to discern and to do God's will, however, they pursued power, fame, and, above all, wealth (66, 69).

RELIGION, SELF-INTEREST, AND RACE

Tocqueville argued at certain points in the *Democracy* that Christianity's influence on American public opinion was the chief factor in preventing majority tyranny. "While the law allows the American people to do everything," he noted, "there are things which religion prevents them from imagining and forbids them to dare" (292). We have now seen, however, that at bottom Tocqueville viewed Americans as virtuous more for selfish than for religious reasons. Did enlightened self-love in fact lead individual Americans to behave justly and honestly and American majorities to respect individual rights? Although Tocqueville reports that most Americans thought that it did, he himself was much less convinced of its efficacy, at least when important matters were at stake.

Tocqueville claims that the doctrine of self-interest properly understood made Americans "orderly, temperate, moderate, careful, and self-controlled" citizens (527). These Americans were good neighbors, politically active, honest, and willing to sacrifice in small ways—all for mostly selfish reasons. Although Tocqueville knew that virtue of this type was not genuine, he thought it had much to commend it, especially when embellished by the residual influence of Christianity. But Tocqueville believed that in difficult cases, when virtue required sacrifice or clearly conflicted with self-interest, enlightened self-love ill served the cause of freedom. This conclusion colors his discussion of American race relations, one of the bleakest parts of the entire *Democracy*.

Tocqueville considered the presence of blacks on American soil the "most formidable evil threatening the future of the United States" (340).[1] The existence of this discrete minority, set apart by "visible and indelible signs," occasioned heinous abuses of majority power (342). Slavery, of course, was the most egregious of these abuses. Tocqueville considered the physical treatment of slaves in the 1830s brutal, but does not dwell on it, choosing instead to focus on the unprecedented crimes against their spirit (317, 361). American slavery, unlike its ancient counterpart, denied its victims "almost all the privileges of humanity" (317). It cut them off from their African heritage, from the blessings of European civilization, from family ties, from opportunities for moral and intellectual improvement, and worst of all, from all hope for freedom and self-respect (317–318, 361–362, 350).

Although most of the Northern states had abolished slavery by the time Tocqueville visited America, free blacks enjoyed few of freedom's fruits. Northern laws discriminated severely against them, and what the laws allowed, public opinion forbade. Thus, with none but phantom rights, they could not vote, sit on juries, benefit from the due process of law, or have any social contact with whites. While intermarriage was permitted, the white spouse of such a marriage was forever disgraced. All in all, the free states seemed to compete with each other to see which could make the lives of their black inhabitants more miserable (350n, 343, 350).

Although Tocqueville described the plight of American blacks most eloquently, his chief concern in analyzing American race relations was to show how slavery and racial hatred endangered the nation as a whole. Tocqueville believed that the sharp cultural differences which existed between Northern and Southern whites as a result of slavery could destroy the Union (374–377). His greater fear, though, was that bloody civil war between the two races would break out, ultimately annihilating one of the two. This was also the "nightmare constantly haunting the American imagination" (358). The outcome of such a war, he predicted, would depend on whether or not the Union survived. If it did, Tocqueville thought the whites' numerical superiority would make them victorious. If the Union dissolved, Southern blacks with "numbers and the energy of despair" on their side would overpower Southern whites, despite their economic and political superiority (358).

What role did Tocqueville give American Christianity in ameliorating this sorry state of affairs? Tocqueville believed that the birth of Christ signaled the eventual end of slavery, an institution which the ancients considered natural and perpetual (439). Christianity opposed slavery by "insisting on the slave's rights," that is by universalizing and sanctifying the principle of equal liberty (348). For more than a millenium slavery retreated as the Christian democratic revolution advanced. Even the Christians who reintroduced slavery to the West in the sixteenth century (an act Tocqueville viewed with abhorrence), considered it an exception to their social system (341, 363).

Tocqueville's initial claim that Christianity shaped America's moral horizon in the early nineteenth century leads us to believe that, in his view, it would play a prominent role in abolishing slavery, if not racial prejudice. Indeed, his traveling companion, Gustave de Beaumont, who wrote extensively on the plight of American blacks, came to precisely this conclusion. In the opening remarks of his essay, "Can Black Slavery Be Abolished in the United States?," he argued as follows:

> . . . let us begin by admitting that in the United States there is a general trend of opinion toward freeing the black race. A number of moral principles combine to produce this effect.
>
> First, religious beliefs, which are spread over all the United States. Several sects show ardent zeal for the cause of human liberty; the efforts of religious men are unceasing and their influence, almost imperceptible, nevertheless makes itself felt. On this subject, one wonders if slavery could last very long in the heart of a Christian society. Christianity means the moral equality of man. Once this principle is admitted, it is difficult not to arrive at the idea of social equality, whence it appears impossible not to go on to political equality (Beaumont 1958, 201–202).

In contrast to Beaumont, Tocqueville analyzes the moral dynamics of American race relations almost exclusively in secular terms. His analysis strongly suggests that, in his view, the sacred conception of rights was no longer normative for Americans of the 1830s. Although rhetorically effective in rallying support for faraway causes requiring no sacrifice (such as the struggle for Polish independence), it fell flat against the hard rock of self-interest (289–290).[2] "Nowadays," Tocqueville observed, slavery must be attacked "from the master's point of view," that is by showing the slaveholders that abolition was in their interest (348). This, at any rate, was how Americans viewed the matter. "In the United States," Tocqueville noted, "people abolish slavery for the sake not of the Negroes but of the white men" (344). Sadly, this was as true in the North where democratic religious idealism once flourished as in the South where it never took root.

Tocqueville first shows that the Northern states abolished slavery for pragmatic reasons. Northern whites were enlightened democrats, the most modern of men who aimed, through their labor, to conquer nature for the sake of their own generalized freedom and prosperity (345–347; see Winthrop 1988, 157). They hated slave societies whose mores were contrary to the work-oriented principles essential to economic success. These include the ideas that freedom makes men productive, that work for profit is honorable, and that material well-being is the main object of existence (345–347, 375–376, 550–551). Also, Northern whites could abolish slavery with little fear that the newly freed blacks, who were small in number, could harm them. Indeed, many of these whites reduced this number further by selling their slaves southward just prior to abolition, a callous and immoral example of enlightened self-interest (350–351).

Tocqueville shows, however, that the advantages of abolition to Southern whites were far less clear. In the long run, he believed, abolition would serve Southern interests if Southern whites wished to embrace modernity. Although climate made slavery more profitable in the South than in the North, American economic history since colonial times invariably taught one lesson: free societies "increased in numbers, wealth, and well-being" more rapidly than slave societies (344, 352). All this was obvious to the more enlightened Southerners.

Yet these facts hardened rather than softened their slaveholding hearts. Southern aristocrats rightly concluded that abolition threatened their antique mores, their political power, and their very physical existence. Although they feared a slave revolt, they concluded, not unreasonably, that it was more dangerous to live among a large, degraded, and hostile population of freed blacks than to perpetuate slavery (360–363).

Tocqueville believed there were only two ways to avoid race war in America: blacks and whites had to separate completely or to mingle completely (355). The only prospect for separation involved emancipation and colonization, a plan supported by prominent American statesmen such as Jefferson and later Abraham Lincoln. Tocqueville liked this plan because, in theory, it could end America's racial conflict as well as provide a foothold in Africa for Christian, democratic principles. Liberia, founded in 1820, already had "a representative system, Negro juries, Negro magistrates, and Negro clergy" (359). He dismissed it immediately, however, as being highly impractical. Blacks constituted more than one-fifth of all Americans in the 1830s, and not even a massive colonization effort could halt the growth of this population. These demographics led Tocqueville to conclude that "the Negro race will never again leave the American continent . . . except by ceasing to exist" (359, 360, 360n).

Tocqueville also assessed the prospects for a free, interracial society. A large mulatto population in certain parts of the United States testified to this possibility, although most mulattoes were conceived under the coercive conditions of slavery (356). While intermarriage was compatible with Christian, democratic principles, and even allowed in some Northern states as we have seen, most whites recoiled from the practice. Furthermore, racial justice would have to be achieved immediately after emancipation to forestall strife. Once free, Tocqueville predicted, blacks would quickly resort to violence if denied their rights. "There is no intermediate state," he wrote, "that can be durable between the excessive inequality created by slavery and the complete equality which is the natural result of independence" (355, 360, 362).

Tocqueville was pessimistic regarding America's chances of becoming a free, interracial society because he believed that racial prejudice generally increases rather than decreases when slavery is abolished. This was certainly the case in the Northern states where, ironically, blacks were hated most "where slavery was never known" (343). This prejudice, which he considered "immovable," arose from differences in origin, education, social condition, and color (317, 343). This last difference, the most critical, would always perpetuate the "memories of slavery," which in turn would always disgrace the race (341).

While Tocqueville locates the origin of American racial prejudice in nature and historical circumstances, he links its staying power to its hold on America's soul. By the 1830s, American public opinion had crystallized around two key ideas which were inconsistent with racial justice. The first was that God's moral laws were ultimately instrumental to the pursuit of self-interest. This was the unmistakable lesson of the doctrine of self-interest properly understood. Tocqueville predicted that American slavery would end because the forces of modernity opposed it, Christianity considered it unjust, and the country's long-term economic interests required freedom (363). But these interests, at least as Americans of the time understood them, did not require that blacks be treated fairly or charitably. Only religion could demand such things, but in Tocqueville's view, the golden age of Christian morality was "already long past" (528).

Anglo-Americans also considered themselves a superior race, set apart from the rest of mankind by their economic and political accomplishments (357). This racial pride, so offensive to Christianity, led the vast majority of whites to treat blacks as less than human and to justify their behavior by arguing away their humanity (see Winthrop 1988, 159). In this way, they successfully shielded themselves from the logical consequences of their Christian, democratic principles.

CONCLUSION

Although Tocqueville considered American Christianity's failure to address racial prejudice a sign of moral weakness, he did not hold churchmen wholly responsible for it. Indeed, he thought they had to accommodate to the selfish, hubristic tendencies of their congregations in order to retain a modicum of influence. Whether he believed these accommodations could preserve even a vestige of Christian morality in the long run is an open question as we shall see in the next chapter.[3] He feared that the same tendencies which led his Americans to oppress blacks would lead their descendants to oppress other minorities until, in the end, no one's rights would be safe. Such were the dangers of linking the idea of rights solely to personal interest (259–261).

CHAPTER EIGHT

FUTURE PROSPECTS

This new society which I have tried to portray and would like to evaluate has only just begun to come into being. Time has not yet shaped its definite form. The great revolution which brought it about is still continuing, and of all that is taking place in our day, it is almost impossible to judge what will vanish with the revolution itself and what will survive thereafter (703).

Tocqueville sought to ascertain the "*natural state*" (his emphasis) of Christianity in democracy in order to establish firm guidelines for effective religious statesmanship (299). "Knowing what we can hope and what we must fear," he remarked, "we can clearly see the aim to which our efforts should be directed" (299). As we have seen, though, the "natural state" of American religion was anything but clear. Outwardly, Americans were highly religious. Christianity was universally respected, the churches flourishing, the Sabbath strictly observed, skeptics silent. Under these circumstances, "the mass of mankind," saw "no impediments to established beliefs" (300).

Tocqueville discerned in the "depths of men's souls," however, that the democratic revolution had gradually, but irrevocably undermined America's traditional faith (300). When measured against its Puritan origins, American Protestantism in the 1830s was quite weak, often operating less as a transcendent faith than as a staple of American public opinion.[1] Its first principles were mainly self-oriented and rational rather than biblical and altruistic. Although American Catholicism was flourishing, it too had imbibed the secular ideas and interests of the majority. Finally, Tocqueville believed that Christianity contributed less to the cause of American freedom than he first suggests. Much American virtue was based on self-interest rather than faith, and slavery, the worst of American evils, seemed impervious to religious influence.

What, in Tocqueville's view, were American Christianity's future prospects in light of these conditions? How vulnerable was this faith to further changes in America's national character? I shall address these questions at the beginning of this chapter. I shall then turn to Tocqueville's strategy for strengthening Christianity and to other, more secular components of his multifaceted plan for preserving freedom. Finally, I shall briefly consider Tocqueville's guarded prognosis for America. Tocqueville believed that successful liberal democracies require high quality statesmanship, but saw no such statesmanship in America's future.

Most scholars agree that Tocqueville's version of Christianity compromised with democracy in order to insure its survival. At the same time, however, they miss the grimness in his assessment of even this modified faith's future. Zuckert and Hinckley are typical in this regard, arguing that he based his hopes for revised Christianity on the constant, natural human desire for immortality (Zuckert 1981, 259, 277, 279; Hinckley

1990b, 40, 48). Galston and Zetterbaum also consider Tocqueville an optimist regarding Christianity's future, but criticize him for underestimating the strength of democracy's secular propensities (Galston 1987, 511; Zetterbaum 1967, 120–121, 123).

I believe, however, that Tocqueville's fears regarding secularization made him quite guarded about Christianity's prospects, even when modified according to his recommendations. His preferred forms of the faith were, in fact, compromised religions in which enlightenment rationalism dominated traditional biblical principles. The future survival of these "mixed regimes" depended on keeping skepticism at bay. Although Western Christianity held its own, for the most part, in the early nineteenth century, Tocqueville believed that, "time, circumstances, and the lonely workings of each man's thought," could in the end "shake or destroy" any democracy's faith (644). Should this occur, an "empty ghost of public opinion" might sustain this faith for a time, but only as a shadow of its former self (644).

Such democracies, Tocqueville feared, would be vulnerable to certain enlightenment doctrines opposed to Christianity in principle. The first was the atheistic "political gospel" which led to the terror and tyranny that discredited France's revolution (see chapter 4, 75). The second was materialism, a soul-denying doctrine which thrives wherever an excessive taste for physical well-being disposes people to believe that matter is all. Its most fertile breeding ground is democracy where gratifying this taste is a top priority (544–545).

The third was pantheism, a monstrous religion which exploits the democratic desire for a simple, unitary, and rational metaphysic (446–447, 486; see, in general, Lawler 1993, 33–50). Pantheism teaches that all things "material and immaterial, visible and invisible" are part of a universal Being "who alone remains eternal in the midst of the continual flux and transformation of all that composes Him" (451, 452). This cosmology rejects the biblical dichotomies between God and His creation, this and the other world, and human and non-human life. By making the species rather than the individual the active agent in history, pantheism destroys personal responsibility and renders human choice meaningless (451, 452).

Tocqueville believed that any or all of these doctrines, if powerful enough, could hasten the slide of lapsed or faint-hearted Christians into some form of tyranny. Their common tendency is to reduce the individual to a cipher, assaulting his pride, his status as a moral agent, and the sanctity of his rights. They also reinforce the democrat's passion for present pleasure while increasing his anxiety about death (448, 544, 548). Under these circumstances, it is very easy for people to surrender their freedom to a traditional despot or to view themselves as sheep and the government, rather than the Lord, as their shepherd (691, 692).

THE FUTURE OF AMERICAN CHRISTIANITY

Tocqueville thought that Christianity would prevent either of these grim alternatives from occurring in America, at least for the foreseeable future. His understanding of America's unique historical development and of mature public opinion generally accounts for this relative optimism (299, 640). Although America experienced a fairly rapid transition from a limited to a mass democracy, she did not undergo a mores-shattering revolution as did France (432). This, plus the country's Puritan founding, made Americans less vulnerable to overtly anti-Christian doctrines than European democrats. Public expressions of atheism were rare in the

United States, and there were virtually no traces of materialistic or pantheistic doctrines (Tocqueville 1959b, 79–80). Finally, the shift of authority within American Christianity from Bible and church leaders to democratic public opinion also occurred gradually, fostering a sense of greater continuity than did in fact exist.

Tocqueville also considered American public opinion highly conservative, appearances to the contrary notwithstanding. "In the United States," he observed, "general doctrines concerning religion, philosophy, morality, and even politics do not vary at all, or at least are only modified by the slow and often unconscious working of some hidden process" (640). This observation beautifully captures Tocqueville's sense of how intransigent Americans were regarding fundamental beliefs, of how this intransigence could, in fact, give way over time, and of how difficult it would be to discern the change. A skeptical majority may look "as if it did believe," except to the eyes of the most perceptive observer (644).

Ironically, Tocqueville thought that some of the same factors which transformed traditional American Protestantism into a civil religion contributed to this latter faith's long-term stability. Pragmatism, for example, made Americans resistant to new ideas, especially in the realm of theology or metaphysics. American English contributed to this tendency by adapting to the country's business-oriented mentality at the expense of the traditional language's "learned, intellectual, and philosophical character" (478–479).

Skepticism also played an odd role in preserving the status quo. Americans clung to their religious opinions not out of deep conviction, but because they doubted the existence of better ones (187, 642). They also took pride in these opinions, considering them a kind of independently acquired intellectual property

(186).[2] Finally, Tocqueville thought negative peer pressure would deter true religious innovators from seeking and acquiring a following. "This circumstance," he noted, "is wonderfully favorable to the stability of beliefs" (643).

Tocqueville feared, however, that in the long run these factors could not help but threaten America's already compromised faith. By the 1830s, pragmatism had made Americans "slaves of slogans" and easy prey for idea mongers who pandered to their privatistic and materialistic inclinations (258, 479, 483). Americans also lived in a "state of perpetual self-adoration" during this time, bridling at the "least reproach" or the "slightest sting of truth" (256). Tocqueville, was utterly put off by this smug self-satisfaction. While acknowledging its stabilizing influence on the then prevalent form of American piety, he knew that at some future time it could further check Christianity's already muted critical voice, 258–259, 643).

Tocqueville was also concerned about the long-term stability of America's metaphysical framework. Although Americans considered themselves Christians in the 1830s, enlightenment rather than biblical imagery shaped their core beliefs as we saw in chapter 5. Virtually all, including the uneducated, saw their common life's work as conquering nature rather than zealously serving Christ (453–454). This idea, or some variation of it, shaped American fantasies as well as American behavior. Thus, people from all walks of life dreamed of "marching through wildernesses, drying up marshes, diverting rivers," and "peopling the wilds," rather than reaping a heavenly reward (485).

This poetic vision was partly responsible for America's remarkable accomplishments in science and technology (453–454). It also led Americans to seek an "absolute good" in this world and to actually consider it within humanity's grasp (453). Tocqueville well knew that utopian ideas of this sort could further reduce religion's influence on the public mind. Those who think themselves naturally good, self-sufficient, and endowed with an "indefinite capacity for improvement" are not likely to be moved by the Christian tale of sin and redemption (374, 452–454).

Tocqueville's final prognosis for the future of American Christianity as for that of Christianity in general was uncertain. "No one can know," he wrote in the last pages of the *Democracy*, "which of the old institutions and former mores will continue to hold up their heads" as democracy matures, "and which will in the end go under" (703). This uncertainty did not, however, prevent him from developing a strategy to prevent the further erosion of faith. As James W. Ceaser put it, there is often a tension in Tocqueville's thought between his "recommendations for helping liberal democracy" and his "analysis of the fragility of his own proposed solutions" (Caesar 1990, 32).

FUTURE RELIGIOUS STATESMANSHIP

Tocqueville believed that the task of preserving and strengthening American piety, such as it was, afforded ample opportunities for creative statesmanship. In his view, America's population in the 1830s contained a small number of out-and-out atheists, some highly vocal religious enthusiasts, and a large number of nominally observant though skeptical Christians (256, 299–300, 534–535). This latter group, which constituted the vast majority, made public opinion distinctly "favorable to religion" (300). Tocqueville thought that future majorities of this sort would ultimately determine American Christianity's fate. The main challenge for future American statesmen was to make "spiritual conceptions" prevail among this group (545).

The strategy Tocqueville recommended to these statesmen was highly conservative. He first advised them to strengthen American Protestantism as it was rather than to attempt to revive the more orthodox versions of the faith or to encourage conversions to Catholicism. Although he considered Catholicism more suited to democracy than Protestantism, as we have seen, he feared the consequences of tampering unnecessarily with prevailing mores. "Do not try to detach men from their old religious opinions in order to establish new ones," he warned, "for fear lest in the passage from one belief to another the soul may for a moment be found empty of faith and love of physical pleasures come and spread and fill it all" (544).

Tocqueville also sternly warned future American statesmen against reinstituting any form of religious establishment. Although "state religions . . . perhaps sometimes momentarily serve the interests of political power," he remarked, they are "always sooner or later fatal for the church" (545; see also 94). At the same time, he opposed giving clergymen political power either directly or indirectly, as we have seen. He was so convinced of the dangers of this course of action that he preferred "shut[ting] priests up within their sanctuaries" to allowing them to be politically active (545–546).

Finally, Tocqueville wished Americans to continue their long-standing practice of promoting Christianity through public education (Tocqueville 1960, 31–32, 47–48).[3] Tocqueville's support for this practice seems odd, given the strength of his feelings about separation, but he apparently did not consider the presence of clergy or Bible reading in public school classrooms a violation of this principle. Indeed, he considered these customs, which had Puritan roots, a clear sign of America's great originality (45). Nor did he seem to mind other forms of government aid to Christianity such as the blue laws, the laws against swearing, and the official days of prayer which were then part of the American scene (Tocqueville 1960, 226). Tocqueville's support for the Puritans' approach to public education did not, however, extend to their educational philosophy. While the Puritans promoted learning to advance their particular brand of Protestantism, Tocqueville wanted his Americans to learn how Christian virtue served their personal and political interests (45, 528–530). Tocqueville argued that enlightened self-love was at bottom a Christian concept as we have seen (chapter 3, 56–57). Although he considered it less intrinsically worthy than religious altruism, he thought it the only principle capable of keeping American public opinion favorably disposed toward faith (529).

Tocqueville's preferred form of religious education would, in the first instance, spell out the link between self-interest and immortality. Moralists could plausibly show, he believed, that religious observance was the best means to satisfy that desire or was at least worth the gamble. His loose citation of Pascal's famous wager expresses this latter thought quite nicely: "If we make a mistake by thinking the Christian religion true, we have no great thing to lose. But if we make a mistake by thinking it false, how dreadful is our case" (529).

The strongest selfish support for American Protestantism in his view, however, was not the desire for immortality which flickered sometimes strongly, sometimes weakly amidst American materialism, but rather the widespread perception of its political utility (548; see Winthrop 1991, 408). In Tocqueville's America the view that Christianity was politically useful was a cardinal tenet of political orthodoxy. It was firmly lodged in the heart of American public opinion, adhered to and proselytized for with a zeal once reserved for theological truths (292–294). "The better to touch their hearers," Tocqueville noted, preachers "are forever pointing out how religious beliefs favor freedom and public order." "It is often difficult to be sure when listening to them," he continued, "whether the main object of religion is to procure eternal felicity in the next world or prosperity in this" (530).

Tocqueville did not consider these popular perceptions a sure-fire guarantee for Christianity's survival, despite the great importance he attached to them. He knew that such perceptions could easily change in a more secular age. He also knew that enlightened self-love could only promote faith among a people capable of deferred gratification, that is of "habitually and effortlessly" sacrificing "the pleasure of the moment" for long-term interests (529). Finally, he knew that skeptics could grow accustomed "not to think about what will happen after their li[ves]," and thus erode the best natural foundation for belief (548). For these reasons, Tocqueville chose not to base his hopes for America's future political health on Christianity alone.

TOCQUEVILLE'S SECULAR STRATEGY

Tocqueville's "new political science" contains a secular strategy for promoting freedom which, like his civil religion, addresses the major pathologies of democracy. A brief discussion of this strategy is needed here in order to put his religious statesmanship in the proper perspective. It is difficult to discern precisely how much Tocqueville relied on religion in his overall plan for preserving freedom. He probably believed that Christianity would always be of some political value, even if its future strength were greatly diminished. It is worth noting, however, that he omits religion entirely when summing up his recommendations for preserving freedom at the end of the *Democracy* (695–702).

The first part of Tocqueville's secular strategy consisted of strengthening the non-religious means for fighting individualism. Here again he relied primarily on the principle of self-interest properly understood. In addition to fostering a certain degree of piety, this principle taught Americans how to profit by fulfilling the positive obligations of citizenship ignored by universalistic Christian morality (Tocqueville 1959, 192; Tocqueville 1955, 12). Tocqueville hoped that in democracies of the future, sacrifice would be linked to "private advantage," patriotism to "greed," and "civic spirit" to the "exercise of political rights" (236–237, 525). In the last analysis, Tocqueville was convinced that good democratic citizenship depended more on teaching people that "individual interest is linked to that of country" than on widespread religious belief (236).

Tocqueville also hoped that enlightened self-love would teach future Americans to value social relationships as much as Americans of the 1830s did. Tocqueville's contemporaries formed a whole slew of voluntary civil associations which enabled them to enjoy many of the varied benefits of modern culture. These included marriage, highly popular social and economic clubs which contributed to the country's prosperity, moral and religious societies which provided a haven from rampant materialism, and political organizations which Tocqueville admired, among other things, for teaching Americans to appreciate civil associations and to use them well (513–517, 520–524, 596–597).

Tocqueville believed that voluntary associations contributed to American freedom in a variety of ways regardless of their purpose. On the most basic level, they checked the inward-oriented tendencies fostered by individualism. "Feelings and ideas are renewed, the heart enlarged, and the understanding developed," Tocqueville argued, "only by the reciprocal action of men one upon another" (515). In a more directly political sense, they provided democratic alternatives to the powerful aristocratic bodies which protected freedom while defending their class interests or doing society's work. In this respect, they served as independent sources of power which could not "be twisted to any man's will or quietly trodden down" (697).

Tocqueville also wanted democratic statesmen to find non-religious means for checking petty, shortsighted materialism. Anchoring people's aspirations to the future was essential to this sort of character building he believed. In a country where "unhappily skepticism and democracy exist together," he wrote, "philosophers and the men in power should always strive to set a distant aim as the object of human efforts; that is their most important business" (548).

Tocqueville thought the appropriate means for undertaking this "important business" would vary according to time and place. Moralists must persuade the public that planning and executing long term political projects has private as well as social benefits. In democracy as elsewhere, "it is only by resisting a thousand daily petty urges that the fundamental anxious longing for happiness can be satisfied" (548). Similarly, leaders must always act with the future in view, linking the political advancement of their subordinates to merit or public service, and showing by example that nothing of value can be achieved without hard work (549).

The final and most critical component of Tocqueville's secular strategy was to promote non-religious alternatives to Christianity's support for rights (699). The first priority here was to protect and strengthen the constitutional safeguards for these rights. These include federalism and local autonomy, the separation of powers and checks and balances, a free press, the forms and formalities of government, and due process of law (162, 509–513, 695–699). Although Tocqueville valued the protection these institutional safeguards offered individuals, he most admired their effect on America's political culture. At a time in history when people often feel isolated and weak and governments strong and self-satisfied, constitutional safeguards enhance the individual's self-respect while humbling the politically powerful (701).

The next task for Americans was to strengthen the already existing link between rights and personal interest. Democrats are more likely to defend their rights when they benefit from them concretely than when called to an abstract duty. As Delba Winthrop points out, however, Tocqueville believed that America's commitment to rights must be more an affair of passion than of intellect. "Interest will never be permanent enough and visible enough to sustain the love of liberty in the hearts of men," Tocqueville wrote in an unedited note on the French Revolution, "if taste does not fix it there" (cited in Winthrop 1991, 422; Tocqueville 1951–, 2(2):345; see also Winthrop 1991, 414–424).

The chief means for fostering this taste, which is more aristocratic than democratic in character, was to make a commitment to rights central to America's sense of honor (Winthrop 1991, 418, 419–424). Thus Americans must learn to respect the rights of the naturally gifted and give them responsibilities commensurate with their talents. They must also take pride in and feel obliged to exercise their political rights—the right to elect public officials, to discuss public business together, to join political associations, to support the authority of government by personal service, and to run for office (509–513, 520–524, 540). In the end, Tocqueville considered political participation the best secular means (and perhaps the best means altogether) for fostering

the instinctive regard for rights essential to their survival (513; Tocqueville, 1955, xiv).

AMERICAN STATESMANSHIP

Tocqueville believed that American statesmen and
moralists were ultimately responsible for guarding and
strengthening our national character. In order for American Christianity to retain its political value, future leaders must be or act like believing Christians and conform
"scrupulously" to religious morality in conducting the
nation's affairs. Only thus can they "flatter themselves
that they are teaching the citizens to understand it and
to love and respect it in little matters" (546). In less
religious times, these leaders must at least "act with the
future in view" and "teach individuals by their example
to conduct their private affairs properly" (548, 549).

For freedom to survive, the American people must
also be as willing and able to "summon men worthy
of public confidence to the direction of affairs" as
they were in the late eighteenth century (197). Then,
Tocqueville observed, America was blessed with statesmen such as Thomas Jefferson, who didn't disregard
public opinion, but shaped it in politically healthy ways.
Jefferson and his ilk had a "greatness all their own"
which "brought honor to the nation" (113–114, 257).
Their moral leadership enabled the people to rise to the
occasion when called upon to fight for independence or
to ratify the Constitution (113–114).

Tocqueville found American public life in the 1830s
dismal by comparison.[4] "The most outstanding Americans are seldom summoned to public office," he lamented, and "the race of American statesmen has
strangely shrunk" (197). Most state politicians, he believed, were little more than ciphers willing to prosti-
tute themselves to the majority in order to feed off of it.
In the U.S. House of Representatives, he remarked,

"one can often look in vain for a single famous man" (200). Although the U.S. Senate was filled with more illustrious characters, not one senator graces the pages of the *Democracy* by name to offer a constructive solution to the nation's most vexing problems (201).[5]

Tocqueville believed that direct popular election was partly responsible for this leadership crisis (201). Although the American people sincerely desired the public good, they were ill-equipped to pursue it properly. Picking virtuous leaders was, in his view, a difficult task which most people have neither the time nor the ability to do well. Thus, "they are bound always to make hasty judgments" and are easily fooled by charlatans (198). Sometimes Americans lacked even the inclination to choose wisely. Worshipping equality, they tired at the sight of "any superiority, however legitimate" and carefully kept the higher classes from power (198). While "not afraid of great talents," Tocqueville notes, they had "little taste for them" (198). Natural aristocrats tended in turn to avoid political careers which required dissembling or self-abnegation (198, 199).

Tocqueville considered the Framers of the Constitution partly responsible for this sorry state of affairs. While recognizing and addressing some of the dangers of excessive majoritarianism, they made a number of serious errors which compromised the prospects for good statesmanship. Most serious was their decision to allow presidential reeligibility, a principle which deprived the nation of executive energy by making the chief executive too dependent on public opinion (137–138).

> Reeligible . . . the President of the United States is only a docile instrument in the hands of the majority. He loves what it loves and hates what it hates; he sails ahead of its desires, anticipating its complaints and bending to its slightest wishes; the lawgivers wished him to guide it, but it is he who follows.

> In this way, intending not to deprive the state of one
> man's talents, they have rendered those talents almost
> useless, and to preserve a resource against extraordi-
> nary eventualities, they have exposed the country to
> dangers every day (138).

In Tocqueville's view, President Andrew Jackson ex-
emplified American statesmanship at its worst.
Tocqueville considered the popular president "a man of
violent character and middling capacities" with virtually none of the qualities needed for governing a free
people (278). In office, he was little more than the
"majority's slave" yielding to "its intentions, desires, and
half-revealed instincts" (393). Although he had the power
to elevate popular mores, he pandered instead to prevailing disunionist sentiments to heighten his personal
prestige (393, 394).

Tocqueville made a variety of proposals for enhanc-
ing the prospects for decent statesmanship. These included strengthening the executive and judicial branches
of government and the national government in relation
to the states (Kraynak 1987, 1190–1193). His hopes
that these suggestions would be adopted by the American people, however, were not very high. In seeking to
restrict popular power for the sake of freedom and good
government, he resembled the Federalist statesmen
whose partial success in moderating democratic excess
was a "lasting memorial to their patriotism and wisdom" (177). His fear was that like these statesmen who
"struggled against the irresistible tendency of their age
and country," he too would suffer defeat at the hands
of more thoroughgoing democrats (176).

CONCLUSION

Tocqueville's fears for the future of American Christianity were part of his sober appraisal of America's

overall prospects as a free society. Although he strongly suggests our republican institutions will be durable at several points in the *Democracy*, he also considered a devastating race war and a dangerous weakening of the national government likely (357–358, 394, 395–400). Either of these eventualities, he thought, could lead to a tyranny of the traditional sort. If one scans the *Democracy* as a whole, however, it becomes clear that, in Tocqueville's view, the most potent long-term threat to American freedom was the "tendency of American society . . . toward ever-increasing democracy" (399). This evil, which threatened all healthy facets of American mores, could exacerbate the dangers of majority tyranny or lead to democratic despotism if unchecked.

Although Tocqueville was sober about the prospects for American freedom, he was not fatalistic. "I have sought to expose the perils with which equality threatens human freedom," he wrote, "because I firmly believe that those dangers are both the most formidable and the least foreseen of those which the future has in store. But I do not think they are insurmountable" (702). Had he thought so, he continues, he would have contented himself with "mourning in secret over the fate of [his] fellows" rather than writing a book like *Democracy in America* (702). Tocqueville believed that America's political well-being hinged to a certain extent on how well future generations learned the lessons of the "new political science" set forth in this book.

CHAPTER NINE

A SUMMING UP

The essence of the lawgiver's art is by anticipation to appreciate [the] natural bents of human societies in order to know where the citizens' efforts need support and where there is more need to hold them back. For different times make different demands. The goal alone is fixed, to which humanity should press forward; the means of getting there ever change (543).

How much light, after all, does Tocqueville shed on American religion and politics? More specifically, how accurate was his assessment of the Puritans' role in shaping American Christianity and America's national character? Did he capture or miss the essence of American faith in the 1830s? How justified were his concerns regarding secularization, and how wise, in view of these concerns, were his recommendations that Christianity make vital concessions to democratic public opinion? Finally, how relevant are Tocqueville's arguments regarding Christianity's political importance to today's moral–political crisis and the critical task of preserving American freedom? I shall conclude my study by addressing these questions.

TOCQUEVILLE AS HISTORIAN

Tocqueville considered the Puritans to be America's founders because of their formative influence on the country's national character, a character that provided vital, continuous support for their principle of equal freedom. Tocqueville initially claimed that the Puritans made America a sort of Christian commonwealth where moral and intellectual life is governed by faith. He later shows, however, that the Puritans set in motion a process which made individual judgment and self-interest the bases of American mores rather than the Bible and Christian love.

Tocqueville explains the ambiguous legacy of Puritanism by analyzing its roots in the Old and New Testaments. In so doing, he implies that, in a sense, the true founders of America were Moses and Christ. Moses gave the Puritans the legalistic, intolerant spirit of religion which made orthodoxy their primary concern. Christ furnished them an egalitarian spirit of freedom which laid the groundwork for America's constitutional democracy and its rights-oriented ethos. Although Tocqueville first suggests that these two "spirits" ruled America harmoniously throughout her history, he later shows that, in fact, they marched in opposite directions (295). This opposition derived from a more fundamental conflict between the democratic and non-democratic elements within biblical Christianity itself.

The dynamic, irreversible nature of the democratic revolution virtually guaranteed that equality would emerge as the dominant element within Christianity and would ultimately come to threaten its very existence. The critical turning point in this chain of events was Luther's invention of a philosophical method which eventually undermined all forms of traditional religious and moral authority including the concept of orthodoxy itself. In America, the Puritans aided the democratic cause by extending the scope of the philosophical method into the realm of politics. This expansion helped transform America from a religiously-oriented society to a secular polity where religion played an important, but subordinate role. By Tocqueville's time, all elements of America's national character had a secular rather than a religious foundation and the Puritan spirit of religion in its undiluted form was almost nowhere to be seen.

In my judgment, Tocqueville's analysis of the Puritans as America's founders stands on its own merits as a plausible, intellectually stimulating account of our origins. His assertion that the Puritans shaped our national character which in turn shaped our national destiny is a needed corrective to the predominant legal–institutional approach to the founding. It also enriches, while not settling, the ongoing scholarly debate between those who see Christianity and those who see political philosophy as the primary source of our regime.

Having made this claim, however, I must add that Tocqueville's discussion of the American founding is weak in some respects. Thomas G. West argues that Tocqueville's rejection of the traditional view of the founding led him to downplay the role of ideas and laws in shaping our country's history and to overemphasize the role of "subpolitical causes" such as equality of conditions and mores. As a consequence, West continues, Tocqueville ignored important statements of political principle in the pre- and post-revolutionary period such as the Declaration of Independence and undervalued the significance of the Constitution (West 1991, 157–160).[1]

West believes that Tocqueville completely misunderstood America's origins and nothing short of a wholly new explanation would satisfy him. He also errs by reducing Tocqueville to a "political sociologist" as I argued in chapter 2. Nonetheless, Tocqueville's analysis often lends itself to this kind of error. While he thought that ideas influence, as well as being influenced by, the course of history, he often failed to explain adequately how this influence manifests itself in particular instances. He could have strengthened his case for a Puritan founding, for example, by pointing more directly to the links between Puritan political theory and early American constitution-alism[2] and, I might add, by exploring the intellectual origins of Puritanism in more depth.[3]

Tocqueville also failed to show concretely how en-lightenment ideas transformed Puritanism and other tra-ditional forms of Christianity into the "reasonable" versions of the faith which existed in the 1830s. Nor did he relate how America came to abandon established religion for the separation of church and state. These latter failures are puzzling in the light of Tocqueville's familiarity with the thought of Thomas Jefferson, a key figure in bringing about these changes (Schleifer 1991, 178; see chapter 5, n. 4).

Finally, Tocqueville failed to stress that America's laws and institutions shaped her mores as well as being shaped by them, although he believed this to be the case (see, for example, 94–95, 136–138; Kraynak 1987, 1188). An explicit discussion of the U.S. Constitution's influence on the American character as he knew it would have properly emphasized this point.

Other critics accuse Tocqueville of overstressing the influence of Puritanism on later American Christianity and thus presenting a "narrow, ahistorical view of Ameri-can religious development" (Butler 1990, 289).[4] This charge also has merit. Tocqueville virtually ignored im-portant events in the early history of American Chris-tianity such as the Anglican renaissance, the rise of denominationalism, and the effects of slavery on Chris-tian belief and practice (Butler 1990, 291).

Tocqueville is charged as well with missing the "richness and diversity" of American Protestantism as it existed in Jackson's day (Goldstein 1975, 20). Scholars making this case cite his failure to treat such varied phenomena as religiously-inspired moral and political crusades, the beliefs and organizational structures of the churches, the relationship between church membership and social class, and the conflicts engendered by sectarianism (Goldstein 1975, 19–20, 26; see also Wilentz 1988, 210).

Their most serious allegation, however, is that he failed to grasp the nature and significance of evangelicalism, a phenomenon historians consider central to any account of early nineteenth-century American religion. (Goldstein 1975, 19, 25–26; Schleifer 1975, 247). Goldstein and Schleifer link his neglect to his personality and his Catholic and European background (Goldstein 1975, 20; Schleifer 1975, 247). Kelly attributes it to his desire not to mar his flattering portrait of American Christianity by describing what he considered an emotionally chaotic and politically destabilizing force (Kelly 1984, 46ff.). All agree that this failure was, in Schleifer's words, one of his "major blind spots" (Schleifer 1975, 247).

It is true that Tocqueville devotes scant attention to evangelical Christianity in his writings and had little respect for it. In fact, he dismissed revivalism in the *Democracy* as a form of religious madness, an inevitable result of the excessive materialism of American society (534–535). Although this omission is serious and regrettable, it does not, in my judgment, invalidate his overall assessment of America's religious horizon.

Tocqueville deserves credit for capturing, as no one else did, the essence of mainline Christianity in the 1830s, that is the various ways it accommodated to

equality in order to insure its survival. Even Jon Butler, whose remarks on Tocqueville are generally critical,
concedes his "remarkable acumen" in comprehending
such phenomena as the "tension between individualism and institutionalism" and the "paradox" of Catholic
republicanism. (Butler 1990, 289; see also Wilentz 1988,
209).

Moreover, Nathan O. Hatch has recently shown that
the evangelical churches in early nineteenth-century
America were even more democratic and more hostile
to traditional religious authority than the established,
mainline churches. Although Hatch does not subscribe
to Tocqueville's view that America's core values in the
1830s were secular, his research supports Tocqueville's
contention that all Protestants during that time considered democratic public opinion rather than the Bible the
ultimate arbiter of truth (Hatch 1989, 9–10, 81, 162).

TOCQUEVILLE ON SECULARIZATION AND THE FUTURE OF AMERICAN CHRISTIANITY

The greatest strength of Tocqueville's analysis, in
my judgment, is the light it shed on America's future
religious development. Tocqueville's Protestants broke
the tie with biblical authority that bound their Puritan
ancestors by accommodating to the prevailing secular
currents within American public opinion in the 1830s.
Traditional Protestantism continued to shape American
mores during this time, however, by giving them a conservative, if not quite a religious, cast. Tocqueville noted
this influence in such diverse areas as education, the
arts (492, 256), sexual morality, and family life in general. The influence of biblical Protestantism on America's
national character lasted long into the future as
Tocqueville predicted it would.

The religious component of American public opinion was further diminished, though, in two historic phases: the first from the end of the nineteenth century through the 1930s, and the second in the 1960s and 1970s. In the first phase, a number of factors such as the increasing diversity of the American melting pot, the triumphs of science, and the gradual popular acceptance of non-Christian beliefs and values made American mores more secular. The symbolic events of this era were the Scopes Trial which legitimized an empirical, anti-biblical approach to understanding human origins, and the end of prohibition (Gausted 1983, 170–172; Hunter 1987, 37–38).

In the second phase, severe disenchantment with America's Protestant-dominated religious and political establishments moved the country into what Sydney E. Ahlstrom has called a "post-Protestant era" (Ahlstrom 1972, 1079). Although no one has yet fully explained this generalized loss of faith, contributing causes include the Vietnam war, rapid technological change, an unprecedented generation gap, and widespread value relativism. Also during this period, mass higher education and the mass media brought an "adversary culture" to the heart of middle America, transforming moral permissiveness from a marginal social phenomenon to a national trend (Kristol 1972, 22–30).

Finally, the Supreme Court completely secularized American public education by reinterpreting the Establishment Clause of the Constitution to prohibit prayer and Bible reading in the schools. These, and other rulings that limited the government's ability to assist religion, eroded the political supports which had bolstered Protestantism in the past (Wald 1987, 116–121).

What effect have these changes in public opinion had on American Christianity today? In answering this question, I shall adopt the generally accepted distinction between the mainline Protestant churches and the conservative or evangelical Protestant churches. The mainline churches, we recall, are those which, in varying degrees, intentionally make their beliefs and practices compatible with the views of the majority. They are heavily influenced by post-enlightenment theology and their major concerns are worldly. The conservative churches seek to uphold the standards of traditional Protestantism against the prevailing worldliness of American life. They emphasize belief over works, the afterlife over this life, and conversion over toleration. I shall first consider the mainline and then the evangelical churches (Wald 1987, 63–64; Roof and McKinney 1987, 6, 79ff., 91).

MAINLINE PROTESTANTISM

By and large, the mainline churches have responded to the new secularism by continuing to deemphasize the theological elements of their faiths. Their current understanding of religious freedom illustrates the extent to which this anthropocentric trend has advanced. The Puritans used religious freedom to discern God's will and to subordinate themselves to it. Tocqueville's Protestants detached religious freedom from revelation and made the rational self the final judge of orthodoxy. Today's mainline Protestants link religious freedom to an individual's feelings, thus virtually detaching the principle from the concept of objective religious truth. Peter L. Berger describes this process as follows:

> Subjective emotionality takes the place of objective dogma as a criterion of religious legitimacy, thus laying a foundation for the "psychologization" of Christianity— and the same process relativizes the religious contents, since the "heart" of one individual may say different

things from the "heart" of another (Berger 1967, 156–157).

With sincerity as their watchword, today's mainline Protestants are much more tolerant than the Protestants of Tocqueville's day. This broadmindedness extends to Catholics, non-Christians, and atheists as well as to fellow Protestants. In contemporary America, it is no longer socially mandatory for anyone to hide his or her skepticism or unbelief. Perhaps the only exceptions to the new tolerance are those who reject the prevailing religious relativism and insist on taking traditional orthodoxy seriously (see Carter 1993).

Although Tocqueville's Protestants were not nearly as biblically minded as their Puritan ancestors, the Bible continued to shape their education, their religious activities, and their leisure. Even those most addicted to worldly gains and pleasures read Scripture every Sunday. The Bible today exerts very little influence on the daily lives of mainline Protestants, perhaps because the "higher critics" have persuaded them over the years that the book is a human rather than a divine creation. Biblical literacy has declined precipitously, as we have seen, and the Bible no longer serves as a primary resource for dealing with life's uncertainties. Even those churchmen who view the Bible as a guide to social action probably turn to social science first when dealing with a problem at hand (542; Gausted 1983, 121ff.; Ahlstrom 1972, 796).

In the new, less biblical versions of Protestantism God is often viewed as an agent of human purposes rather than as their final end. Thus, many mainline churches aim not to please Him, but to help Christians attain comfort, success, and, most of all, relief from anxiety. To be a Christian, in this view, means to become authentic, to attain mental health, or to belong to a caring community rather than to attain salvation through grace. Today one rarely hears talk about hell or damnation from the mainline pulpits, and the rosy view of human nature fostered by equality has supplanted the old Protestant notion of human sinfulness (Bellah 1985, 228–230).

The decline of biblical authority has also reduced the importance of the theological issues which historically divided Protestants and gave their churches distinct religious identities. These issues include questions about episcopal authority, free will and predestination, the efficacy of sacraments, etc. Although the mainline American churches traditionally downplayed matters of dogma, church members still considered these matters significant until recently (Marty 1976, 76). While most mainline Protestants affiliate with a particular denomination today, their knowledge of and concern for what once made that denomination unique is marginal at best. Caplow and his associates could not find a "flicker of interest" among the laypeople of a typical American community for the doctrinal differences which ostensibly made them members of one church rather than another (Roof and McKinney 1987, 77; Caplow et al. 1983, 286).

Although Protestant clergymen in the 1830s were no match in influence for their Puritan predecessors, they still exerted considerable religious authority over their flocks. The same cannot be said of the mainline clergy today. The new, more subjective approach to faith has led to a dramatic increase in "religious individualism." This is the tendency among mainline Protestants (and many other Americans) to define their own relationship with God using Bible, church and clergy perhaps as resources, but not as authoritative guides. Thus, most laypeople feel no overriding commitment to their churches, no obligation to abide by their teachings, and no compunction about leaving if their churches fail to live up to their expectations (448–449; Roof and McKinney 1987, 32; Gallup and Castelli 1989, 44, 252).

The voluntary nature of contemporary church membership has also led to a "marketing" situation in which public opinion both inside and outside the churches becomes dominant. Within the churches, authorities shape doctrines and practices to suit the collective preferences of their congregations establishing a *de facto* system of governance known as "religious populism." This form of democracy is a far cry from Puritan congregationalism where God's word rather than consumer demand was dispositive. Church authorities also cater to what is more broadly fashionable when recruiting new adherents. America's pluralistic environment requires this, forcing them to compete not only with other churches, but with secular organizations whose functions resemble their own (Roof and McKinney 1987, 249; Berger 1967, 137–145).

When Protestant clergymen taught Christian morality in Tocqueville's day, they prudently supported only those Christian principles compatible with democracy. Today, the mainline churches generally adopt this rule, espousing nothing in the New Testament which blatantly contradicts the American Creed. While the churches then generally avoided political controversy to preserve their strength, the mainline churches now are more likely to jump into the fray. Overall, mainline involvement in social issues has led, as Tocqueville predicted it would, to considerable disaffection among those who oppose their church's positions (Roof and McKinney 1987, 27; Bellah 1985, 230; *Democracy*, 297; Wald 1987, 32).

Mainline Protestantism's response to the sexual revolution shows how pliable its interpretation of Christian morality can be. Traditional Christianity's sexual code required virginity outside of marriage, continence and fidelity within marriage, and the strict avoidance of all forms of license. The Puritans enforced these laws with a zeal Tocqueville thought excessive despite his general admiration for their ethos. Although sexual morality in Tocqueville's day was grounded more in self-interest than in biblical precepts, it received considerable support from the churches and the level of chastity was high. Both the Puritans and Tocqueville's Protestants also generally enforced the biblical injunctions which subordinated women to men within the family, the churches, and society as a whole (43, 291, 590–591, 600–603).

In today's America, however, it is no longer a "point of honor" to be chaste. American public opinion now tolerates extramarital sex as well as other sexual attitudes and practices offensive to the biblical God. The broadly-based drive for sexual equality has also transformed American life making any form of male dominance suspect. By and large, the mainline churches have accommodated to, if not embraced, these revolutions. Indeed, mainline Protestantism itself has been influenced by the feminist movement, allowing women ordination in some cases and greater participation in religious affairs generally (622; Greeley 1989, 91; Gallup and Castelli 1989, 195).

Tocqueville predicted that American Protestantism would gradually lose strength over time as a result of its inherent defects and the general incompatibility of biblical religion with democracy. The accuracy of this prediction, as it applies to the mainline, did not become evident until the late 1960s when most of the major mainline churches stopped their long, uninterrupted period of growth and began to shrink. The loss in membership was accompanied by a drop in financial contributions, missionary work, and other less tangible signs of church vitality such as religious conviction. Roof and McKinney predict that the mainline Protestant establishment will continue to decline in size, social power, and influence as we enter the next century (Kelley 1986, 1–10; Roof and McKinney 1987, 233).

AMERICAN CATHOLICISM TODAY

In contrast to mainline Protestantism, the American Catholic church seems to be thriving. The number of American Catholics has grown steadily throughout this century and now constitutes between 21 and 28 percent of the country's entire population. (Greeley 1990, 31, 109; Roof and McKinney 1987, 230). If this growth trend persists, Gallup and Castelli suggest that over the next four decades Catholics could outstrip Protestants as the dominant religious group in America (Gallup and Castelli 1989, 23; Roof and McKinney 1987, 237). This data seems to confirm Tocqueville's judgment that Catholicism has greater intrinsic appeal to democrats than Protestantism (450).

For the most part, however, the American Church has followed the mainline Protestant churches in deferring to rather than shaping American public opinion. Since the Second Vatican Council democratized Catholicism's ecclesiastical structure, the American Church has experienced a "social and theological fracturing" which makes "any deduction from first principles largely irrelevant." This fracturing is reflected both in Catholic theology which is more "do it yourself" than not, and in ritual where the "abandonment of old-style uniformity" is "virtually complete" (Sullivan 1990, 34; Roof and McKinney 1987, 56). Most American Catholics consider their faith as much a "sensibility" as a revelation and thus open to the most varied subjective interpretations (Sullivan 1990, 33, 35).

American Catholics, as Tocqueville describes them, were a devout, somewhat intolerant minority who cherished their dogma and accepted church authority without question (Tocqueville 1985, 50). Today's Catholics, however, are more interested in the "valuable relationship network" and "schedule of benefits" offered by church membership than in a "faith, chosen for its truth" (Sullivan 1990, 36). The generalized "ease in the world" they experience comes from widespread acceptance by American society, concessions to American materialism and public opinion generally, and a decision to remain Catholic on their own terms (Greeley 1989, 47; Sullivan 1990, 34). What they lack, however, is the "spiritual growth" and "refuge" from modernity that even Tocqueville's American Catholics enjoyed to a limited extent (Sullivan 1990, 34–35).

EVANGELICAL PROTESTANTISM

Tocqueville's analysis of the future of American Protestantism does not seem to account for the recent rise of Protestant fundamentalism. This conservative form of Protestantism, commonly known as evangelicalism, appears to be firmly grounded in traditional Protestant theology. Despite some significant differences within the evangelical movement, all believe that the individual must unconditionally submit to God's will, that the Bible is the inerrant word of God, that Christ is divine, and that a conversion ("born again") experience is essential for salvation. These beliefs create a strong commitment to orthodoxy among evangelicals and a strong sense of transcendent purpose (Baumer 1989, ix, x; Wald 1987, 63).

According to most objective accounts, American evangelicalism is thriving. Evidence of this vitality includes a sharp increase in the number of evangelical churches, educational institutions, outreach programs, and ministers; a growing sense of unity and coherence within the churches and in national evangelical organizations; growing political strength and social acceptance; and a general sense of militancy and triumphalism. These trends have led to a "seismic shift" in American religion, moving the balance of power within American Protestantism clearly in the conservative direction (Roof 1983, 133–134).

James Davison Hunter's recent book *Evangelicalism: The Coming Generation* provides substantial support for Tocqueville's views on the future of American Protestantism however. Hunter argues that the evangelical churches are now gradually and almost unconsciously conforming their core beliefs and values to secular public opinion despite their strenuous attempts to resist its encroachments. In theology, these accommodations include softening the doctrine of biblical inerrancy, subjectivizing some aspects of traditional Protestant orthodoxy, and a greater tolerance for the beliefs and prospects of non-Christians. Their reasons for making these accommodations include a desire for acceptance by mainstream America, a splintering of opinion regarding theological issues within the evangelical camp, and, most important, a growing discomfort with the cognitive demands of biblical faith (Hunter 1987, 31–49).

Hunter also contends that the evangelical churches frequently cross the moral boundaries which separate them in theory from the mainline churches. This is most evident, he believes, in their current preoccupation with the self. Until recently, evangelicals accepted the traditional Protestant view of the self as weak, inherently sinful, and hostile to religious ideals. Now, however, they tend to view the self more positively, treating it as something of ultimate worth and significance. Thus, they are more prone than their ancestors to self-love, self-involvement, and the selfish pursuit of wealth. They have also redefined sin in sexual and family matters, moving from patriarchy toward androgyny and embracing some of the milder aspects of the sexual revolution. Although these accommodations have not yet completely eroded traditional Protestant morality, Hunter believes that this is likely to occur in the not too distant future (Hunter 1987, 60–62, 64–65, 71ff., 93–106).

Hunter predicts that if these trends continue the odds that evangelicalism will maintain its integrity in America's secular milieu are not very high. His pessimism, like Tocqueville's, is based on the premise that modernity offers little support for true biblical religion and that orthodox churches which choose to participate fully in American life must pay the Devil his due. This payment, for the evangelicals, consists of accepting majority opinion in moral and intellectual matters not intentionally, but by a sort of cultural osmosis. It also consists of changing, ever so subtly and gradually, the meaning of orthodoxy itself. If the payment has already been made, as Hunter contends, the resistance of American Protestantism to democracy is at an end and the further secularization of American life is well-nigh inevitable (Hunter 1987, 161–163, 180–186, 193, 201–202, 210–213).

A CRITIQUE OF TOCQUEVILLE'S CIVIL RELIGION

Tocqueville often praises traditional religion in the *Democracy* and genuinely thought that certain of its elements were essential to America's political health. He especially sought to preserve those parts of traditional Christian theology, such as its future-oriented ethos, which opposed the excessive individualism and selfish materialism fostered by the spirit of freedom taken to an extreme.

In the end, though, Tocqueville clearly admired American moralists for weakening traditional Christianity. He considered the Mosaic Code the law of a "rough, half-civilized people" with no right to rule a faith which would be politically useful (42). When the concern for orthodoxy governed Europe, it fostered an aristocratic morality incompatible with democratic freedom. The powerful and rich talked much about virtue and in some cases even practiced it, but did very little for the common good (525). During this time, the European masses were superstitious, deferential, otherworldly, and even content, but hardly good citizens (28, 530, 619). Although the American Puritans democratized Christianity considerably, their Judaized version of the faith produced too little freedom and too much of the zealotry and excessive moralism which Tocqueville found so offensive to the democratic spirit (42–43).

Tocqueville also admired these moralists for linking Christianity to self-interest properly understood, a mainstay of majority opinion which he considered the "best suited of all philosophical theories to the wants of men in our time" (527). American piety, in his view, was based less on sincere belief than on the common perception that religion served public as well as private purposes. Tocqueville considered this linking of piety to interest a stroke of genius despite his doubts about its long-term viability. Although most Americans of the 1830s were not traditional Christians, they were generally good citizens who cherished their rights and respected the rights of others. The glaring exception to this, of course, was the behavior of white Americans towards blacks and Indians.

Pierre Manent considers Tocqueville's attempt to link Christianity to perceived utility the "central difficulty" of his religious statesmanship. The difficulty, as he describes it, is this: religion's power over people's souls depends on the quality of their attachments to it. It can only thrive, and hence be useful in addressing the spiritual ills of democracy if people consider it true.

When skeptics are self-consciously religious for selfish reasons as Tocqueville's Americans were, religion's moral efficacy becomes inextricably linked to subjective assessments of interest. As Manent put it, "the religion of Americans loses its own utility in proportion to which they become attached to it because of that utility" (Manent 1982, 121, 125, 128–129; my translation).[5]

I shall assess this criticism by reflecting on the changes which have occurred in popular American morality since Tocqueville wrote, beginning with black–white relations. Tocqueville considered American racism impervious to the ethical mix of enlightened self-love and modified Christian morality. Thus, he predicted, as we recall that whites and blacks would never live together on any condition resembling equality. Ironically, Tocqueville was unduly pessimistic in this regard. Although race relations have been and continue to be America's most serious domestic problem, the country has clearly achieved greater racial justice and harmony than Tocqueville thought possible.

Tocqueville erred in this regard because he underestimated the range of moral resources available to Americans fighting racial injustice. He ignored the evocation of a just God in early American public documents, the nascent Christian abolitionist movement of the 1830s, and the almost religious reverence with which large segments of American public opinion regarded the Union as an instrument of freedom. Although he foresaw that great crises could produce great democratic statesmen, he never imagined that a man such as Lincoln could fundamentally alter the course of American history by using a religiously-informed public philosophy against slavery and national disintegration. Nor could he foresee that a century later a black religious leader, Martin Luther King, Jr., would turn public opinion against the worst forms of racial prejudice by drawing on these same principles.

Unfortunately, Tocqueville's fears regarding the long-range capacity of American faith to bolster personal morality against the excesses of equality were more well-founded. As a result of the decline in religious belief and the depreciation in its public status, we are now threatened by many of the evils he so eloquently identified and opposed. The demands of Americans for material gratification seem ever more insatiable, the American idea of rights has expanded in scope while becoming dissociated from duty, and selfish individualism has weakened America's once powerful network of voluntary associations. These changes have adversely affected our public life as well. There is no more distressing feature in American politics today than the almost total absence of public virtue both inside and outside of government. As Irving Kristol trenchantly noted a number of years back, "Self-government, the basic principle of this republic, is inexorably being eroded in favor of self-seeking, self-indulgence, and just plain aggressive selfishness" (Kristol 1973, 27).

The inadequacy of America's unique synthesis of Christianity and enlightened self-love can be seen most graphically in the area of sexual morality. This is one area, ironically, where Tocqueville was wrongheadedly optimistic. Although he is widely admired for his almost uncanny ability to predict future political events, he failed to foresee the sexual revolution which has transformed the moral landscape of our time. Indeed, Tocqueville never seriously doubted the long-term effectiveness of America's solution to the problem of license.

In recent years, however, we have witnessed an unprecedented increase in promiscuity, adultery, rape, and other forms of sexual behavior relatively rare in Tocqueville's day. Although a slight rise in chastity has accompanied the AIDS epidemic and the recent growth of religious fundamentalism, the prevailing sexual ethic is one of almost complete relativism.

Tocqueville believed that the principle of self-interest properly understood would replace Christianity as the bulwark of American sexual morality. The long-term efficacy of this principle, however, required that both sexes continue to reap tangible benefits from being chaste. In contemporary America the connection between chastity and self-interest, at least as Tocqueville understood it, is tenuous at best. Although acquiring wealth still demands a certain single-mindedness, it no longer forecloses possibilities for extramarital affairs. Indeed, these possibilities have multiplied exponentially as the social and economic barriers separating men and women have crumbled and sex has become increasingly independent of love. The old equation of sexual morality and national economic prosperity also no longer holds as the sexual revolution now fuels a significant part of the American economy.

In America of the 1830s, women could not violate traditional sexual mores without risking public disgrace. Despite appearances to the contrary, Tocqueville thought that democratic public opinion regarding deeply held moral principles would be highly conservative (640). His assessment of American attitudes toward sexual behavior was correct for several generations after he wrote. Until the 1960s, these attitudes were relatively stable and, as a consequence, women continued to regard chastity as a "point of honor" (622). By the early 1970s, however, the American public came to tolerate broad deviations from chastity as a result of the weakening of its traditional supports. At the present time, the forces which shape American values—the universities, the media, and the arts—encourage license with far more vigor than they ever promoted restraint.

In today's America, sexual freedom has merged with a swollen individualism to seriously endanger traditional family life. Tocqueville thought our ancestors had secured marriage against individualism by making it a voluntary association whose end was private happiness. This strategy certainly succeeded for many generations after he wrote. But the current high incidence of divorce attests to the ultimate fragility of marriage when grounded solely on subjective assessments of well-being.

CONCLUSION

Tocqueville was well aware of the shortcomings of mainline American Christianity. He knew, for example, that secularization could further weaken this faith leaving American morality in a rather wretched state. He also knew that no version of Christianity which emphasizes rights over duties and conciliates rather than opposes selfish individualism could ever allay the restlessness and melancholy bound to afflict its skeptical and hypocritical adherents. Finally, he knew that a certain amount of deception is involved in promoting civil religion, a certain willingness on the part of statesmen and moralists to promulgate religious doctrines they consider doubtful or untrue. The best argument for Tocqueville's advocacy of just such a religion however, is its reasonableness when compared to the alternatives. History suggests that religion may be necessary for freedom and that only a "civil" form of Christianity can meet that need.

Most traditionalists believed that biblical religion should provide the politically sanctioned authority which governs American moral and intellectual life. Tocqueville considered orthodoxy and political power a dangerous mix, and no historical development since that time has proved him wrong. Tocqueville also believed that democrats think in ways that render the traditional biblical faiths incapable of serving their metaphysical needs. While they naturally hope for life after death, they generally doubt its existence or at least long for it less than for earthly goods.

Liberals start from the premise that private rational judgment should be the ultimate principle of authority in a free society. In Tocqueville's view, however, this principle failed to create the free, autonomous human beings it promised and brought instead the rule of secular public opinion with its potential to enslave and degrade. This insight, more than anything else, led him to recommend American Christianity as a useful model for modern democracies. History also supports Tocqueville's position here. There are no past or present examples of a large, free society without religiously-based popular morality. Nor is there a country which has actively sought to eradicate religion that has not nestled under a tyrant's heel.

Tocqueville thought that the chief tasks of statesmanship in any epoch were to strengthen those elements of a nation's character which bolster freedom and to curb those elements which undermine it. Although he does not speak directly to current policy questions in America, he does offer some guidance to those who would preserve a political role for American Christianity today. This guidance, as it relates to contemporary issues, is as follows:

1. Religious functionalists should encourage nondiscriminatory public support for our most common religious values. In practical terms, this means fighting to preserve the still-extant links between religion and government, supporting new policies like a mandatory moment of silence in the public schools, and restoring a form of civic education which stresses the religious

dimension of our political history and principles. Such policies must respect religious diversity without sacrificing the mild biblical morality which still forms an important strand of our national character.

2. Religious functionalists should support candidates for public office who respect religion or are sincerely religious themselves. Such candidates, it goes without saying, must not be shysters who simply pander to public opinion, but ethical statesmen genuinely willing and able to oppose the excessive egalitarianism endemic to American life. Deciding which individuals can serve the public interest in this way is no easy matter, for as Tocqueville pointed out, discerning character in politics requires an almost philosophical wisdom.

3. Finally, religious functionalists should show contemporary clergymen the merits of teaching virtue from the pulpit while personally staying aloof from electoral politics. In doing so, the clergy must learn somehow to walk a fine line between accommodating the ideas and interests of their congregations and sacrificing the core moral principles of their faiths. The clergy should also stress the selfish benefits of religious observance. Ironically, American religion has declined in strength partly because people are no longer convinced of its usefulness. At the same time, however, it has become more necessary than ever (Manent 1982, 129).

Even if we grant that piety in America is politically desirable, it remains highly questionable whether a functionalist approach to strengthening it can succeed. This is especially true when the practitioners of this approach as well as large numbers of Americans are skeptics or lukewarm believers. Tocqueville once compared statesmen to navigators whose realm of action is strictly limited by forces beyond their control (163). This metaphor seems aptly to describe the plight of would-be religious reformers today. The changes wrought by mod-

ern American democracy in science, commerce, the relations between the sexes, education, and, above all
public opinion, may have made even a modest strengthening of religion out of the question.

Tocqueville denied, however, that irresistible forces
could prevent democratic statesmen from fostering the
essential prerequisites of freedom. In fact, he wrote
Democracy in America to convince the best of them
that the fate of freedom was in their hands (705). Yet
Tocqueville also knew that statesman had to modify
their strategies for strengthening freedom according to
changing conditions. "Different times," he wrote, "make
different demands" (543, see also 12). He did not,
therefore, intend his reflections on American Christianity to be rigid prescriptions for the future, but rather,
starting points for discussion and thought. Such
ponderings should consider the various non-religious
strategies Tocqueville recommends for promoting freedom. These strategies are especially important if bol-
stering religion under present circumstances is no longer
feasible.

Tocqueville, as we know, was a liberal, albeit of a
new kind. Those seeking to protect, and perhaps improve, the liberal way of life can learn much from his
writings about faith and the modern world. While warning traditionalists that Christianity needs freedom to
flourish, he admonishes liberals to support and respect
religion lest they needlessly weaken freedom. Both sides
in today's culture war would do well to heed his advice.

NOTES

PREFACE

1. My translation of passages from Tocqueville's correspondence will be noted in the text. All other citations from this correspondence will include the source of the English translation and of the French original.

CHAPTER ONE

1. All references to *Democracy in America* are to Tocqueville, 1969. Parenthetical references in the text are to this edition by page number alone.

2. Tocqueville and Beaumont arrived in New York on May 11, 1831 and left New York on February 20, 1832 (Jardin 1988, 101). On June 29, Tocqueville discussed religion extensively in a letter to his good friend Louis de Kergolay (Tocqueville 1985, 45–59; Tocqueville 1951–, 13(1): 225–238). This letter, which describes America's felicitous combination of democracy, religion, and freedom, is an indispensable source for understanding his analysis of American faith. Tocqueville's travel diaries also contain significant entries on religion. These appear in Tocqueville 1960. James T. Schleifer argues correctly, I believe,

that Tocqueville's early views on the nature of American religion changed little during the nine years when he was writing the *Democracy.* "As early as the end of June 1831," Schleifer notes, " . . . his travel diaries and letters home refer to nearly all of the key themes relating to religion which would later appear in the 1835 and 1840 portions of his book" (Schleifer 1982, 303). See also chapter 3, note 2.

3. One prominent exception is Robert Bellah, et al., *Habits of the Heart* (1985). This book treats religion as well as other facets of contemporary American life from a Tocquevillian perspective (Bellah 1985). Cushing Strout's *The New Heavens and the New Earth* (1974) in an ambitious attempt to relate the history of religion and politics in America to Tocqueville's political thought.

4. William J. Bennett reports that between 1960 and 1990 there has been "a 560 percent increase in violent crime; more than a 400 percent increase in illegitimate births; a quadrupling in divorce rates; a tripling of the percentage of children living in single-parent homes;" and "more than a 200 percent increase in the teenage suicide rate" (Bennett 1993, i).

5. Hunter refers to traditionalists as "cultural conservatives" or "moral traditionalists" and liberals as "liberals" or "cultural progressives." He argues that the current political conflict in America between these two groups has replaced a more traditional form of conflict in which different religious bodies clashed over issues of doctrine, observance, and church organization. Thus, while orthodox Catholics and Protestants were antagonists for much of American history, they now consider their theological differences less important than their common commitment to biblical morality and to a biblical worldview. This commitment unites them, orthodox Jews, and certain conservative secular intellectuals against today's liberals (Hunter 1991, 42–43, 45–46, 121–122).

6. The term "religious functionalist" is a variant of "functional traditionalist," a term used by William A. Galston to describe someone who argues for morality on the basis of "asserted links between certain moral principles and public

virtues or institutions needed for the successful functioning of a liberal community" (Galston 1991, 280).

7. Three contemporary Christian religious functionalists are Stephen L. Carter, Richard John Neuhaus, and Glenn Tinder. See Carter 1993, 161, Neuhaus 1984, ix–x, and Tinder 1989, 2. Neuhaus was a Lutheran in 1984, but recently became a Roman Catholic. More reticent religious functionalists include Robert Bellah, Walter Berns, William A. Galston, and Irving Kristol. See Bellah et al. 1985, Berns 1986, Galston 1991, and Kristol 1991.

8. This essay first appeared in *Daedalus* 1967, 96:1 (Winter):1–21. It is reprinted with many other fine essays on American civil religion in Richey and Jones 1974.

9. Bellah refers to "general civil religion" as "the lowest common denominator of church religions" (Bellah 1976, 57). Rouner sees American civil religion as "a means whereby Christian loyalties and values have been indigenized and become effective in a modern, pluralistic society" (Rouner 1986, 128). John Murray Cuddihy defines American civil religion as the "religion of civility" or "the social choreography of tolerance" that exists at the core of today's mainline faiths (Cuddihy 1978, xiii, 2).

10. For a highly informative overview of the civil religion debate, see Mathisen 1989. This essay also contains an excellent bibliography of civil religion scholarship written between 1967 and 1988 (Mathisen 1989, 141–146).

11. According to Kenneth D. Wald, the mainline religious groups in America today include the Congregationalists, Methodists, Episcopalians, Presbyterians, Disciples of Christ, American Lutherans, American Baptists, Unitarians, and Friends. The evangelical groups include the Missouri and Wisconsin Synod Lutherans, Southern Baptists, the Churches of Christ, and the Assemblies of God. These lists are not exhaustive (Wald 1987, 64). See also Roof and McKinney 1987, 85–91.

12. Carl Becker, Louis Hartz, and Thomas L. Pangle are among the scholars who give Locke preeminence (Becker 1942; Hartz 1955; Pangle 1988). J.G.A. Pocock points to classical

republicanism as the intellectual source of the Founding, while Garry Wills looks for our roots in the "Scottish Enlightenment" (Pocock 1975; Wills 1978).

13. See, for example, the work of Harry V. Jaffa, John P. Diggins, and Ellis Sandoz (Jaffa 1984; Diggins 1986; Sandoz 1990).

14. Andrew C. McLaughlin first made this claim in 1932 (McLaughlin 1932, 3ff.).

15. Edmund S. Morgan, for example, considers these convenants the bases for our belief in the principles of limited government, delegated power, and popular rule (Morgan 1965, xliii–xlvii). Daniel J. Elazar connects them to the idea of federalism, which, in his view, permeates all aspects of American politics (Elazar 1988, 14). Donald S. Lutz traces the U.S. Constitution's debt to colonial charters and state constitutions which were covenant oriented (Lutz 1988). While agreeing with Lutz that the covenant tradition shaped early American politics, Joshua Miller argues that the Framers rejected this version of politics out of hostility to direct democracy, its dominant principle (Miller, J. 1991).

Perry Miller asserts with regard to our national character that American messianism has its roots in the Puritans' tendency to view their New England societies as models for the entire Christian world to emulate (Miller, P. 1964, 1–15). Philip J. Greven believes that the childrearing patterns of evangelical Puritans are a major source of the traditional American distaste for tyranny (Greven 1977, 17, 338, 339). Sacvan Bercovitch suggests that Puritan political sermons, or jeremiads, helped to create American capitalism and its middle class ethos (Bercovitch 1978, xii–xv, 18, 27–29). William G. McLoughlin contends that the Puritans gave America a tension-ridden "culture core" consisting of dualisms between freedom and social order, reason and intuition, and realism and idealism (McLoughlin 1978, 25, 35, 41).

16. Kristol believes that secularization is but a phase of American intellectual history that is rapidly coming to an end. He predicts that traditional Christianity will soon come to play a more central role in American life (Kristol 1991 22, 25–26).

CHAPTER TWO

1. Tocqueville wrote the following to his friend and protégé Artur de Gobineau on October 2, 1843: "Je ne suis pas croyant" ("I am not a believer") (Tocqueville, 1951–, 9:57; my translation).

2. Other scholars who consider Tocqueville a skeptic include James W. Ceasar, Robert Eden, Ralph C. Hancock, John C. Koritansky, Robert P. Kraynak, Peter A. Lawler, Jack Lively, Pierre Manent, Marvin Zetterbaum, and Catherine H. Zuckert. See Ceasar 1990, Eden 1990, Hancock 1991, Koritansky 1990, Kraynak 1987, Lawler 1993, Lively 1962, Manent 1982, Zetterbaum 1967, and Zuckert 1981.

3. Lukacs translates Tocqueville's October 2, 1843 letter to Gobineau in Tocqueville 1959, 204–210, but omits the passage cited above in note 1.

4. References to the *Pensées* are to Pascal 1941. The "Pensée" referred to in the text precedes the colon and the page number of the reference in this edition follows the colon.

5. Keohane 1980 describes Augustine's influence on Pascal as follows: "Saint Augustine's primary importance for political philosophy, in France as elsewhere, lay in the vivid political imagery of the *City of God*. This book held a special fascination for Pascal and several other Jansenists. The community of the faithful, sojourning according to the Founder's plan toward its glorious establishment 'in the fixed stability of its eternal seat,' provided a paradigm of a true community for these men" (183–184).

6. References to the *City of God* are to Augustine 1950. The book referred to in the text precedes the colon and the chapter follows the colon.

7. See chapter 6 of Deane 1963 ("Church, State, and Heresy") for an extended discussion of Augustine's views on religious coercion and how they evolved. Keohane 1980 discusses Louis XIV's treatment of the Jansenists on 263–264.

8. References to the *Persian Letters* are to Montesquieu 1949a. The "Letter" referred to in the text precedes the colon, and

the page number where the reference appears in this edition follows the colon. The translations are mine. References to *The Spirit of the Laws* are to Montesquieu 1949b. The book referred to in the text precedes the colon and the chapter follows the colon. For a more detailed analysis of Montesquieu's religious–political views, see Kessler 1983 and Pangle 1973, 249–259.

9. All references to Rousseau in the next several paragraphs are to Book IV, Chapter 8 of *On the Social Contract*. For general discussions of Rousseau's civil religion, see Gildin 1983, 180–190; Koritansky 1990, 399; and Zuckert 1981, 262–263.

10. Tocqueville says of this doctrine: "Being within the scope of everybody's understanding, everyone grasps it and has no trouble bearing it in mind" (526).

11. Peter A. Lawler provocatively argues that Tocqueville was indebted above all to Pascal for his understanding of freedom and the human condition generally. Lawler's analysis emphasizes the influence of the "existentialist" as opposed to the Christian Pascal on Tocqueville (see Lawler 1993).

12. As Lamberti put it, "In his published work he does not deal with theology or even religion, but only with the political and moral functions of religion" (Lamberti 1989, 158).

13. Lawler seems to agree with Goldstein that Tocqueville considered Christianity true, but only in the sense that it sheds light on the human condition and addresses certain human needs, and not as a transcendent faith which emphasizes sinfulness, a personal God, orthodoxy, and salvation (Lawler 1993, 3, 92–93, 143–145, 129, 168, 192 n. 7). The Christian principle which Lawler's Tocqueville emphasizes is that "all human beings, not just a few, have souls or spiritual longings" (Lawler 1993, 168). See also Galston 1987, 505–506.

14. Jardin was commenting skeptically here on the possibility of Tocqueville's "deathbed conversion."

15. These include Ceasar 1990, Eden 1990, and Hennis 1991. Lawler considers Tocqueville a political philosopher of

the first rank, but not a philosopher *per se* (Lawler 1993, 98, 114, 159). Tocqueville's rejection of the philosophic life, he argues, was based on his belief in the greater capacity of political life to relieve the "miserable anxiety" which self-conscious humans experience when pondering the human condition (Lawler 1993, 8, 107–108, 109–110, 7, 92–93).

16. Tocqueville wrote to Madame Swetchine in 1857: "The appearance of the problem of human existence preoccupies me incessantly. I can neither penetrate into this mystery, nor detach my eyes from it" (cited in Boesche 1987, 186; Tocqueville 1951–, 15(2):314–315).

CHAPTER THREE

1. For other discussions of the relationship between poetry and religion in Tocqueville's thought, see Lawler 1991, 106–109 and Hancock 1991, 362–366.

2. Catherine H. Zuckert argues that Tocqueville changed his mind between 1835 and 1840 regarding the proper scope of democratic religion and the best way to maintain it. In Volume 1 of the *Democracy*, Zuckert's Tocqueville advised France that the separation of church and state is the key to promoting a full-bodied Christianity. In Volume 2, however, he downplays the significance of separation, advising French churchmen instead to water down their faiths in deference to democratic sensibilities. Tocqueville was less sanguine about European Christianity in 1840, according to Zuckert, because he concluded that America's piety was due more to her unique history (her Puritan background and political stability) than to anything else, and that democrats in general were too skepti-cal to sustain traditional Christian beliefs (Zuckert 1992, 22, 25–27, 29–30).

I think that Tocqueville's views on these matters in Volume 2 complement rather than contradict his views in Volume 1. Tocqueville in 1840 advocated the separation of church and state as vigorously as he did in 1835, and his advice in Volume

2 regarding the necessity of accommodating to democratic skepticism was based at least in part on his earlier analysis of American religion (374, 397, 448–449, 545–546). Tocqueville was also fully aware in 1835 of the significance of American history in shaping American faith (32, 46–47, 288). See also chapter 1, note 2 above.

3. Tocqueville makes a similar point in a letter to Kergolay on August 4, 1857 in which he criticizes Thomas a Kempis' *The Imitation of Jesus Christ:*

> It is not *healthy* to detach oneself from the earth, from its interests, from its concerns, even from its pleasures, when they are honest, to the extent the author teaches; and those who live according to what they read in such a book cannot fail to lose everything that constitutes public virtues in acquiring certain private virtues. A certain preoccupation with religious truths which does not go the point of absorbing thought in the other world, has therefore always seemed to me the state that conforms best to human morality in all its forms (Tocqueville 1985, 357; Tocqueville 1951–, 13(2): 328).

4. Zetterbaum claims here that "Tocqueville is virtually indifferent to the particular tenets professed by this or that democratic society."

5. Tocqueville's few explicit references to Judaism in *Democracy in America* are highly unflattering (see 42–43, 199).

6. Tocqueville's criticism of Islam here applies to Judaism as well.

7. "There are in the entire world," he wrote to Gobineau in 1843, "few religions with such morbid consequences as that of Mohammed" (Tocqueville 1959, 212; Tocqueville 1951–, 9:69).

8. Scholars disagree about Tocqueville's intentions in linking the triumph of democracy to divine providence. Lukacs suggests, for example, that Tocqueville did in fact believe that

the democratic revolution was divinely inspired (Tocqueville 1959, 28). Zetterbaum argues that Tocqueville's "inevitability thesis" was a "salutary myth" designed to persuade aristocrats to support democracy rather than a statement of his true convictions. According to this view, Tocqueville considered the triumph of democracy desirable, but not inevitable (Zetterbaum 1967, 17, 19, 21). I think Tocqueville considered the triumph of democracy inevitable, but wholly explicable in rational terms as he suggests in this passage. I further think he incorporated this novel view of divine providence into his civil religion in order to provide an explanation of history more compatible with democratic sensibilities than the biblical view of the matter.

9. Galston 1987 and Biddiss 1970 discuss this correspondence.

10. I do not here enter into the larger question of Tocqueville's overall intellectual debts. As Peter A. Lawler points out, the foundation of his thought is peculiarly elusive (Lawler 1989). Most scholars who comment on the matter consider Montesquieu the thinker who exerted the greatest influence on Tocqueville (see, for example, Ceasar 1990, 68; Lamberti 1989, 239, 242; Cohler 1988, 170–190). Those favoring Rousseau include (in addition to Koritansky) Hennis 1991, 40, 42, 44, 46 and Bloom 1980, 135–137. Other candidates for Tocqueville's chief teacher include Aristotle or the classics in general (Salkever 1990, 245–262; Zetterbaum 1967, 143; Eden 1990, 379–387) and Pascal (Lawler 1993).

11. Tocqueville describes American women, Allan Bloom remarks, "as though they had been educated by Rousseau" (Rousseau 1979, 24).

CHAPTER FOUR

1. In the *Recollections*, Tocqueville formulates his view of history as follows:

"For my part I hate all those absolute systems that make all the events of history depend on great first causes linked together by the chain of fate and thus succeed, so to speak, in banishing men from the history of the human race. Their boasted breadth seems to me narrow, and their mathematical exactness false. I believe *pace* the writers who find these sublime theories to feed their vanity and lighten their labours, that many important historical facts can be explained only by accidental circumstances, while many others are inexplicable. Finally, that chance, or rather the concatenation of secondary causes, which we call by that name because we can't sort them all out, is a very important element in all that we see taking place in the world's theatre. But I am firmly convinced that chance can do nothing unless the ground has been prepared in advance. Antecedent facts, the nature of institutions, turns of mind and the state of mores are the materials from which chance composes those impromptu events that surprise and terrify us (Tocqueville 1971, 78).

2. Roger Boesche gives the following examples of Tocqueville's more or less accurate predictions:

The rise of the United States and Russia as the two dominant superpowers; the political tensions and occasional revolts resulting from black Americans seeking equality; the near annihilation of North America's Native American population; the unification of Germany only by force of Prussian arms; the persistent influence of the English aristocracy despite the hopes of other liberal thinkers; the murderous war between France and Algeria that followed from the French pattern of colonization; the gradual centralization of governmental and private economic power, . . . ; the growing feelings of isolation and powerlessness that have become the concern of so many twentieth century writers; and finally, and most dramatically, his public prediction of France's 1848 revolution less than one month before its eruption (Boesche 1983, 79).

3. See chapter 3, note eight.

4. See especially Federalist 10, 47–51, 62–63, 70–72, and 78.

5. Tocqueville's other, longer definition of the term "mores" is as follows:

> I . . . mean the term "mores" (moeurs) to have its original Latin meaning; I mean it to apply not only to "moeurs" in the strict sense, which might be called the habits of the heart, but also to the different notions possessed by men, the various opinions current among them, and the sum of ideas that shape mental habits.

> So I use the word to cover the whole moral and intellectual state of a people (287).

6. Goldstein 1975 provides a valuable account of Tocqueville's attempts to implement his religious–political principles in France during the years of the July Monarchy and the Second Republic. See especially her chapters 3 and 4.

CHAPTER FIVE

1. Tocqueville emphasizes the separation of church and state so strongly in accounting for America's religious health in the 1830s, writes Goldstein, "that it sometimes takes on the appearance of a *deus ex machina* (Goldstein 1975, 22).

2. Tocqueville's analysis of the Puritans is barely mentioned in the two best general accounts of his thought. These are Lively (1962) and Zetterbaum (1967). It is briefly discussed in Koritansky 1986 (26–28, 30, 56, 144); Koritansky 1990 (390–392); Kraynak 1987 (1183–1184, 1186, 1188); Manent 1982 (131, 133); and Hancock 1991 (376–384).

3. Hatch points out that neither Luther nor Calvin thought of allowing the people themselves to interpret the Bible or to approach it as a source of authority without the guidance of theology and clergy (Hatch 1989, 179–180).

4. Tocqueville's failure to mention Jefferson in relation to the separation of church and state in America is especially strange. As Goldstein points out, he presents disestablishment as "the consequence of a deliberate sociological judgment on the part of the American clergy, rather than as the result of specific historical events and developments" (Goldstein 1975, 24).

5. John Locke first set forth the doctrine of religious individualism in *A Letter on Toleration*. See Locke 1968, 81, 83 and Kessler 1985, especially 490–491. As I have argued elsewhere (Kessler 1983), Jefferson was heavily indebted to Locke for his religious–political principles. In fact, Jefferson used the notes he took on Locke's *Letter* as the basis for his "Bill for Establishing Religious Freedom" (see Sandler 1960).

6. As Jefferson described it, the statesmanship required to disestablish the Anglican Church in Virginia involved the "severest contests" he had ever encountered. Although the Virginia constitutional convention of May, 1776 declared "it to be a truth and a natural right, that the exercise of religion should be free," the efforts of those supporting religious freedom for the next ten years were only partially successful. Prior to the passage of the bill, Jefferson noted, a person "brought up in the Christian religion" residing in Virginia could be subject to increasingly harsh penalties for denying "the Christian religion to be true, or the scriptures to be of divine authority." According to the common law still in effect at the time, he could also be burned for heresy (Jefferson 1944, 41, 273–274).

After the passage of the bill, no one in Virginia could be forced to attend religious services, to support a church financially, or to suffer any civil loss because of his religious beliefs. Despite an attempt in the legislature to limit the religious freedom provided to Christians, the bill when passed comprehended "within the mantle of its protection, the Jew and the Gentile, the Christian and Mahomentan, the Hindoo and Infidel of every denomination" (Jefferson 1944, 47). This "universal" protection of opinion was based on the premise that the sacred and secular realms are separate and distinct (Jefferson 1944, 47). "Our civil rights have no dependance [sic] on our religious opinions," Jefferson wrote in the preamble to the bill, or as he stated more pungently in the *Notes on the State of Virginia*, "It does me no injury for my neighbor to say there are twenty gods, or no God. It neither picks my pocket nor breaks my leg" (Jefferson 1950, 2:545–547; Jefferson 1944, 275).

7. Hatch 1989 presents strong historical evidence to support Tocqueville's observations here. He argues that American Christianity experienced rapid and dramatic democratization from 1780–1830, the years of the early republic (Hatch 1989, 3–6). In his view, the fundamental changes that took place during this time include: 1) a widespread rejection of learned theologians and traditional orthodoxies, 2) a breakdown in the distinction between clergy and laymen, 3) a generalized assertion of the primacy of individual conscience, or the right of individuals to think and act for themselves, and 4) a corresponding elevation of public opinion as a primary religious authority (Hatch 1989, 9, 14, 35, 77, 81, 162, 182).

8. One of Tocqueville's interlocutors, a Mr. Spencer, attributed America's high level of toleration to the "extreme diversity of sects" (Tocqueville 1960, 31).

9. Tocqueville describes this process of opinion formation as follows:

> Men with equal rights, education, and wealth, that is to say, men who are in just the same condition, must have very similar needs, habits, and tastes. As they see things in the same light, their minds naturally incline to similar ideas, and though any one of them could part company with the rest and work out his own beliefs, in the end they all concur, unconsciously and unintentionally, in a certain number of common opinions (640–641).

10. A Mr. Stewart provided Tocqueville with the following example of such ostracism:

> A doctor is clever, but he has no faith in the Christian religion. However, thanks to his ability, he gets a good

practice. No sooner is he introduced into a house than a zealous Christian, a clergyman or another, comes and seeks out the head of the family and says to him: "Be careful of that man. Perhaps he will cure your children, but he will seduce your daughters or your wife; he is an unbeliever. But here, on the other hand, is Mr. So-and-so who is as good a doctor as the other and who is also religious. Trust me and entrust the health of your family to him." Such advice is almost always followed (Tocqueville 1960, 79).

11. Lawler argues that Tocqueville admired his American contemporaries for sharing on some level his own religious skepticism: "He ranks the Americans much higher than most human beings, certainly higher than satisfied aristocrats or devout Christians. He understands them so well because he shares so much in common with them. His description of their restlessness, anxiety, and unhappiness, their despair at not possessing more, could hardly be criticisms. They are, in a human sense, praise. . . . The true greatness of the Americans is in their misery" (Lawler 1990, 410–411).

12. Tocqueville records the following breach of the principle of separation in his "Alphabetic Notebook 1:"

Mr. Richard, a Catholic priest, has been sent to Congress by a Protestant electorate. Mr. Neilson, a Protestant, has been sent to the Commons in Canada by a Catholic electorate. Do these facts prove that religion is better understood or that its power is enervated? They prove, I believe, both one and the other (Tocqueville 1960, 208).

13. Hinckley argues, however, that Tocqueville wanted the French Catholic Church to become more Protestant as its American counterpart did in order to "coexist harmoniously with modern equality" (Hinckley 1990, 341). In her view, as we have seen, the changes he recommended did not touch the core of the revealed faith.

CHAPTER SIX

1. According to Delba Winthrop, Tocqueville believed that the "idea of rights" was aristocratic rather than democratic in origin (Winthrop 1991, 395, 419). While Tocqueville's claim that Americans took "the idea of individual rights" from the "English aristocracy" provides some support for her argument, it is not conclusive (677). Winthrop must explain where English aristocrats got their notion of rights. Since the England which influenced early American development was very much a Christian country, one could argue that her aristocrats distorted a principle which was both Christian and democratic (See 45–46; also Tocqueville 1836, 165–166).

Hancock suggests that Tocqueville reveals his own skepticism regarding the truth of the Christian principle of equal rights by discussing this principle in a chapter which exposes the weakness of general ideas (Hancock 1991, 368–371; see 437–441).

2. Tocqueville here seems to make Luther the accurate interpreter of the New Testament despite his own seeming preference for Catholicism.

3. Tocqueville claimed that by the 1830s, the people had removed the last, vestigial obstacles to their rule. As he described it:

> In the United States in our day the principle of the sovereignty of the people has been adopted in practice in every way the imagination could suggest. . . . The people reign over the American political world as God rules over the universe. It is the cause and the end of all things; everything rises out of it and is absorbed back into it (60).

4. I shall discuss the plight of American blacks, which Christianity did little to relieve, in chapter 7.

5. Despite the importance Tocqueville attributed to female chastity, the portions of the *Democracy* dealing with this subject are among the least discussed and least understood parts of the

book. Ever since John Stuart Mill in 1840 dismissed Tocqueville's views on "democratic morals" as not being "of any considerable value," scholars have either ignored this material entirely or referred to it only in passing (Mill 1963, 244). For a fuller discussion of Tocqueville on sexual morality, see Kessler 1989.

6. Tocqueville suggested that America's national government would most likely consolidate its authority if it were ultimately responsible for regulating questions of mixed sovereignty and if America were involved in "great and frequent wars" (365–366, 677).

7. Robert Nisbet argued several years ago in "The New Despotism" that America is well on the way to becoming a democratic despotism (Nisbet 1975). The best short fictional account of a democratic despotism is "Harrison Bergeron" by Kurt Vonnegut, Jr. (Vonnegut 1983).

8. Although Tocqueville doesn't dwell on America's self-understanding of its relationship with God, he shows that Americans of the 1830s felt obliged to promote the Christian "idea of rights" throughout the world. This is evident from an anecdote he tells about a political meeting he attended in a great, unnamed American city in favor of Polish independence. At this meeting, a clergyman addressed the audience as follows:

> Almight God! Lord of Hosts! Thou who didst strengthen the hearts and guide the arms of our fathers when they fought for the sacred rights of their national independence! Thou who didst make them triumph over a hateful oppression and didst grant to our people the blessings of peace and of liberty, look with favor, Lord upon the other hemisphere; have pity upon a heroic people fighting now as we fought before for the defense of these same rights! Lord, who hast created all men in the same image, do not allow despotism to deform Thy work and maintain inequality upon the earth . . . (289).

This meeting in fact occurred in Boston on September 12, 1831. The speaker was the Congregational minister, Lyman

Beecher (Pierson 1938, 357–361). Tocqueville's placement of the anecdote at the end of a lengthy discussion of American Catholicism and his use of the word "prêtre" (priest) conveys the impression that the clergyman giving the address was Catholic. His intention here may have been to underscore his point that Catholicism is compatible with a democratic, rights-oriented philosophy. This anecdote also belies to a certain extent Tocqueville's assertion that American clergymen were apolitical. Although the priest in the anecdote may abstain from divisive political controversies, he enthusiastically supports commonly held political principles.

CHAPTER SEVEN

1. Other treatments of Tocqueville's analysis of black–white relations include Winthrop 1988, Lerner 1987, and Richardson 1991.

2. Tocqueville also believed that Christianity had little effect on the treatment Americans afforded Indians. Consider the following remarks from his journal:

> The Americans of the United States do not let their dogs hunt the Indians as do the Spaniards in Mexico, but at bottom it is the same pitiless feeling which here, as everywhere else, animates the European race. This world here belongs to us, they tell themselves every day: the Indian race is destined for final destruction which one cannot prevent and which it is not desirable to delay. Heaven has not made them to become civilised; it is necessary that they die. Besides I do not at all want to get mixed up in it. I will not do anything against them: I will limit myself to providing everything that will hasten their ruin. In time I will have their lands and will be innocent of their death. Satisfied with his reasoning, the American goes to the church where he hears the minister of the gospel repeat every day that all men are brothers, and that the Eternal Being who has made them all in like image,

has given them all the duty to help one another (Tocqueville 1960, 200–201; see also *Democracy*, 321–340).

3. Shortly after arriving in America, Tocqueville expressed this concern as follows: " . . . up to what extent can the two principles of individual well-being and the general good in fact be merged? How far can a conscience, which one might say was based on reflection and calculation, master those political passions which are not yet born, but which certainly will be born? That is something which only the future will show" (Tocqueville 1960, 211).

CHAPTER EIGHT

1. "In my opinion," Tocqueville wrote to Kergolay in 1847, "the march of time, the developments in well-being, . . . have in America, taken away from the religious element three-quarters of its original power" (Tocqueville 1985, 193; Tocqueville 1951–, 13(2):210).

2. Tocqueville made this observation when discussing the freedom of the press.

3. The following entries appear in Tocqueville's journal:

a. From a conversation with Mr. Spencer, July 17–18, 1831

Q. Do the clergy control public education with you?

A. Completely. I know of only two exceptions in the State of New York. That seems to me nature's way.

....

Q. How do you manage about public education?

A. The State has special funds of (gap in manuscript) set aside for this purpose. It makes grants from this fund to the local authorities who need them, in proportion to the efforts they promise to make on their own behalf (Tocqueville 1960, 31–32).

b. From a conversation with Mr. Dwight, September 16, 1831

> ... everyone tacitly assumes that education will be moral and religious. There would be a general outcry, something like a popular rising, against anyone who wanted to introduce a contrary system, and everyone would agree that it were better not to have education than to have it given in that way. It is from the Bible that all our children learn to read. . . . (Tocqueville 1960, 47–48).

4. The best historical study of the politics of the Jackson years is Meyers 1960.

5. Tocqueville's bleak assessment of American statesmanship may have been colored by his meeting with Daniel Webster which Pierson describes as a "disaster." "Webster, like thousands of statesmen, cares only for power," Tocqueville remarked shortly after this meeting (Pierson 1938, 393–394). He did suggest, however, that great democratic statesmen could emerge in times of crisis. "At such times," he wrote, "great characters stand out in relief like monuments at night illuminated by the sudden glare of a conflagration. Then genius no longer hesitates to come forward, and the people in their fright forget their envious passions for a time" (199). These remarks are quite prescient in view of Lincoln's rise to power during the pre-Civil War years.

CHAPTER NINE

1. Tocqueville was aware that his American contemporaries venerated the Declaration of Independence. See Pierson 1938, 181–182.

2. Scholars have recently made a plausible, if not wholly convincing claim, for example, that Puritan covenant theology was an important source for the Declaration of Independence and early American constitutionalism (Elazar 1988, 10–11; Lutz 1988, 6–7, 168).

3. A discussion of the role played by British political thought and by Calvinism in shaping Puritan belief and practice would have added much to Tocqueville's account. For an overview of the relationship between American Puritanism and Calvinism, see Hall 1987, 1–16.

4. Butler proposes that "we attach less importance to Puritanism as the major force in shaping religion in America and more importance to the religious eclecticism that has long been prominent." In his view, "the eighteenth century may have left a far more indelible impression on the American religious tradition than did the seventeenth century" (Butler 1990, 2).

5. John Stuart Mill describes the problem with defending religion on utilitarian grounds in the following way:

> "An argument for the utility of religion is an appeal to unbelievers to induce them to practice a well-meant hypocrisy, or to semibelievers to make them avert their eyes from what might possibly shake their unstable belief, or, finally, to persons in general to abstain from expressing any doubts they may feel, since a fabric of immense importance to mankind is so insecure at its foundations that men must hold their breath in its neighborhood for fear of blowing it down" (Mill 1958, 45).

WORKS CITED

Ahlstrom, Sydney E. 1972. *A Religious History of the American People*. New Haven and London: Yale University Press.

Anastaplo, George. 1991. On the central doctrine of *Democracy in America*. In *Interpreting Tocqueville's Democracy in America*. Ed. Ken Masugi, 425–461. Savage, Maryland: Rowman and Littlefield Publishers, Inc.

Augustine, Saint. 1950. *The City of God*. trans. Marcus Dods, D.D. New York: Random House.

Baumer, Randall. 1989. *Mine Eyes Have Seen the Glory: A Journey Into the Evangelical Subculture of America*. New York and Oxford: Oxford University Press.

Beaumont, Gustave de. 1958. *Marie: or, Slavery in the United States: A Novel of Jacksonian America*. Stanford, Calif: Stanford University Press.

Becker, Carl. 1942. *The Declaration of Independence: A Study in the History of Political Ideas*. New York: Alfred A. Knopf.

Beitzinger, A. J. 1984. Pascal on justice, force, and law. *The Review of Politics*. 46 (2):212–243.

Bellah, Robert N. 1989. Comment. *Sociological Analysis* 50:2, 147.

———. 1976. The revolution and the civil religion. In *Religion and the American Revolution*, 55–73. Philadelphia: Fortress Press.

———. 1974. Civil religion in America. In *American Civil Religion*. Eds. Russell C. Richey and Donald G. Jones, 21–44. New York: Harper and Row Publishers, Inc.

Bellah, Robert N., Richard Masden, William M. Sullivan, Ann Swidler, and Steven M. Tipton. 1991. *The Good Society.* New York: Alfred A. Knopf.

———. 1985. *Habits of the Heart: Individualism and Commitment in American Life.* Berkeley: University of California Press.

Bennett, William J. 1993. *The Index of Leading Cultural Indicators.* I Washington, D.C.: Empower America, The Heritage Foundation, and Free Congress Foundation.

Bercovitch, Sacvan. 1978. *The American Jeremiad.* Madison, Wisconsin: The University of Wisconsin Press.

Berger, Peter L. 1983. From the crisis of religion to the crisis of secularity. In *Religion and America: Spiritual Life in a Secular Age.* Eds. Mary Douglas and Steven Tipton, 14–24. Boston: Beacon Press.

———. 1967. *The Sacred Canopy: Elements of a Sociological Theory of Religion.* Garden City, N.Y.: Doubleday Anchor.

Berns, Walter. 1986. Religion and the founding principle. In *The Moral Foundations of the American Republic.* Ed. Robert H. Horwitz, 204–229. Charlottesville: University Press of Virginia.

Biddis, Michael D. 1970. Prophecy and Pragmatism: Gobineau's Confrontation with Tocqueville. *The Historical Journal.* XIII (4): 611–633.

Bloom, Allan. 1990. Western civ and me: An address at Harvard University. *Commentary* 90 (2):15–21.

———. 1980. The study of texts. In *Political Theory and Political Education.* Ed. Melvin Richter, 113–138. Princeton: Princeton University Press.

Boesche, Roger. 1987. *The Strange Liberalism of Alexis de Tocqueville.* Ithaca: Cornell University Press.

————. 1983. Why could Tocqueville predict so well? *Political Theory.* 11:79–103.

Butler, Jon. 1990. *Awash in a Sea of Faith: Christianizing the American People.* Cambridge, Mass. and London, England: Harvard University Press.

Caplow, Theodore, Howard M. Bahr, Bruce A. Chadwick, and Dwight W. Hoover. 1983. *All Faithful People: Change and Continuity in Middletown's Religion.* Minneapolis: University of Minnesota Press.

Carter, Stephen L. 1993. *The Culture of Disbelief: How American Law and Politics Trivialize Religious Devotion.* New York: Basic Books.

Ceaser, James W. 1990. *Liberal Democracy and Political Science.* Baltimore and London: Johns Hopkins University Press.

Cohler, Anne M. 1988. *Montesquieu's Comparative Politics and the Spirit of American Constitutionalism.* Lawrence, Kansas: University Press of Kansas.

Cuddihy, John Murray. 1978. *No Offense: Civil Religion and Protestant Taste.* New York: The Seabury Press.

Deane, Herbert A. 1963. *The Political and Social Ideas of St. Augustine.* New York: Columbia University Press.

Diggins, John P. 1986. *The Lost Soul of American Politics.* Chicago and London: The University of Chicago Press.

Dillenberger, John and Welch, Claude. 1954. *Protestant Christianity Interpreted Through Its Development.* New York: Charles Scribner's Sons.

Eden, Robert. 1990. Tocqueville and the problem of natural right. *Interpretation: A Journal of Political Philosophy* 17 (3):379–387.

Elazar, Daniel J. 1988. *The American Constitutional Tradition.* Lincoln and London: University of Nebraska Press.

Gallup, George Jr. and Jim Castelli. 1989. *The People's Religion: American Faith in the 90's.* New York: Macmillan Publishing Company.

Galston, William A. 1991. *Liberal Purposes: Goods, Virtues, and Diversity in the Liberal State.* Cambridge, England: Cambridge University Press.

———. 1987. Tocqueville on liberalism and religion. *Social Research.* 54:500–518.

Gausted, Edwin Scott. 1983. Did the fundamentalists win? In *Religion and America: Spiritual Life in a Secular Age.* Eds. Mary Douglas and Steven Tipton, 169–178. Boston: Beacon Press.

Gildin, Hilail. 1983. *Rousseau's Social Contract: The Design of the Argument.* Chicago and London: The University of Chicago Press.

Goldstein, Doris. 1975. *Trial by Faith: Religion and Politics in Tocqueville's Thought.* Amsterdam: Elsevier Scientific Publishing Company.

Greeley, Andrew M. 1990. *The Catholic Myth: The Behavior and Beliefs of American Catholics.* New York: Charles Scribner's Sons.

———. 1989. *Religious Change in America.* Cambridge, Mass. and London: Harvard University Press.

Greven, Philip J. 1977. *The Protestant Temperament: Patterns of Child-Rearing, Religious Experience, and the Self in Early America.* New York: Alfred A. Knopf.

Hall, David D. 1987. "On common ground: The coherence of American Puritan studies." *William and Mary Quarterly,* Third Series, 44:193–229.

———. 1978. "Understanding the Puritans." In *Religion in American History: Interpretive Essays.* Eds. John M. Mulder and John F. Wilson. Englewood Cliffs, N.J.: Prentice-Hall, Inc.

Hancock, Ralph C. 1992. Tocqueville on the good of American Federalism. In *Tocqueville's Political Science: Classic Essays*. Ed. Peter A. Lawler, 133–155. New York and London: Garland Publishing, Inc.

———. 1991. The uses and hazards of Christianity in Tocqueville's attempt to save democratic souls. In *Interpreting Tocqueville's Democracy in America*. Ed. Ken Masugi, 348–393. Savage, Maryland: Rowman and Littlefield Publishers, Inc.

Hartz, Louis. 1955. *The Liberal Tradition in America*. New York: Harcourt, Brace.

Hatch, Nathan O. 1989. *The Democratization of American Christianity*. New Haven: Yale University Press.

Hennis, Wilhelm. 1991. In search of the "new science of politics." In *Interpreting Tocqueville's Democracy in America*. Ed. Ken Masugi, 27–62. Savage, Maryland: Rowman and Littlefield Publishers, Inc.

Herberg, Will. 1974. America's civil religion: What it is and whence it comes. In *American Civil Religion*. Eds. Russell C. Richey and Donald G. Jones, 76–88. New York: Harper and Row Publishers, Inc.

Hinckley, Cynthia J. 1990a. Tocqueville on religion and modernity: Making Catholicism safe for liberal democracy. *Journal of Church and State*. 32 (2):325–341.

———. 1990b. Tocqueville on religious truth and political necessity. *Polity*. 23 (1):39–52.

Hooker, Thomas. 1956. "A true sight of sin." In *The American Puritans: Their Prose and Poetry*. 153–164. Ed. Perry Miller. Garden City, N.Y.: Doubleday Anchor.

Hunter, James Davison. 1991. *Culture Wars: The Struggle to Define America*. New York: Basic Books.

———. 1987. *Evangelicalism: The Coming Generation*. Chicago and London: The University of Chicago Press.

Jaffa, Harry V. 1984. "Were the founding fathers Christian?" *This World* 8:3–7.

Jardin, André. 1988. *Tocqueville: A Biography.* Trans. Lydia Davis (with Robert Hemenway). New York: Farrar, Straus and Giroux, Inc.

Jefferson, Thomas. 1950–. *The Papers of Thomas Jefferson.* Ed. Julian P. Boyd, 20 vols. to date. Princeton, N.J.: Princeton University Press.

———. 1944. *The Life and Selected Writings of Thomas Jefferson.* Eds. Adrienne Koch and William Peden. New York: The Modern Library.

———. 1905. *The Writings of Thomas Jefferson.* 20 vols. Eds. Andrew Adgate Lipscomb and Albert Ellery Bergh. Washington, D.C.: Thomas Jefferson Memorial Association.

Kelley, Dean M. 1986. *Why Conservative Churches Are Growing: A Study in Sociology of Religion.* Macon, Ga.: Mercer University Press.

Kelly, George Armstrong. 1984. *Politics and Religious Consciousness in America.* New Brunswick: Transaction Books.

Kelly, George Armstrong. 1983. Faith, freedom, and disenchantment: Politics and the American religious consciousness. In *Religion and America: Spiritual Life in a Secular Age.* Eds. Mary Douglas and Steven Tipton, 207–228. Boston: Beacon Press.

Keohane, Nannerl O. 1980. *Philosophy and the State in France: The Renaissance to the Enlightenment.* Princeton: Princeton University Press.

Kessler, Sanford. 1992. Tocqueville's Puritans: Christianity and the American Founding. *The Journal of Politics.* 54 (3):776–792.

———. 1989. Tocqueville on Sexual Morality. *Interpretation.* 16 (3):465–480.

————. 1985. John Locke's Legacy of Religious Freedom. *Polity.* XVII (3):484–503.

————. 1983a. Locke's Influence on Jefferson's 'Bill for Establishing Religious Freedom'. *Journal of Church and State.* 25 (2):231–252.

————. 1983b. Religion and liberalism in Montesquieu's *Persian Letters. Polity.* XV (3):380–396.

————. 1977. Tocqueville on civil religion and liberal democracy. *The Journal of Politics.* 39 (1):119–146.

Koritansky, John C. 1990. "Civil religion in Tocqueville's *Democracy in America.*" *Interpretation* 17:389–400.

————. 1986. *Alexis de Tocqueville and the New Science of Politics.* Durham, North Carolina: Carolina Academic Press.

Kraynak, Robert P. 1987. "Tocqueville's constitutionalism." *American Political Science Review,* 81:1175–1195.

Kristol, Irving. 1991. "The future of American Jewry." *Commentary,* 92 (2):21–26.

————. 1973. *On the Democratic Idea in America.* New York: Harper and Row Publishers, Inc.

Lamberti, Jean-Claude. 1989. *Tocqueville and the Two Democracies.* Trans. by Arthur Goldhammer. Cambridge, Mass. and London, England: Harvard University Press.

Lawler, Peter A. 1993. *The Restless Mind: Alexis de Tocqueville on the Origin and Perpetuation of Human Liberty.* Lanham, Maryland; Rowman and Littlefield Publishers, Inc.

————. 1991. Democracy and pantheism. In *Interpreting Tocqueville's Democracy in America.* Ed. Ken Masugi, 96–120. Savage, Maryland: Rowman and Littlefield Publishers, Inc.

————. 1990. Was Tocqueville a philosopher? *Interpretation.* 17 (3):401–414.

————. 1989. Tocqueville's elusive moderation. *Polity.* 22 (1):181–189.

Lerner, Ralph. 1987. *The Thinking Revolutionary: Principle and Practice in the New Republic.* Ithaca and London: Cornell University Press.

Lively, Jack. 1962. *The Social and Political Thought of Alexis de Tocqueville.* Oxford: Clarendon Press.

Locke, John. 1968. *Epistola de Tolerantia: A Letter on Toleration.* Trans. J. W. Gough. Oxford: Clarendon Press.

Lukacs, John. 1961. Comment on Tocqueville article. *French Historical Studies* 2:123–125.

Luther, Martin. 1957. "The Freedom of a Christian." In *Luther's Works*, Vol. 31. Ed. Helmut T. Lehman. Philadelphia: Muhlenberg Press.

Lutz, Donald S. 1988. *The Origins of American Constitutionalism.* Baton Rouge and London: Louisana State University Press.

Manent, Pierre. 1982. *Tocqueville et la Nature de la Democratie.* Paris: Juliard.

Marty, Martin E. 1976. *A Nation of Behavers.* Chicago and London: The University of Chicago Press.

Mathisen, James A. 1989. Twenty years after Bellah: Whatever happened to American civil religion. *Sociological Analysis.* 50:2 129–146.

McLaughlin, Andrew C. 1932. *The Foundations of American Constitutionalism.* New York: New York University Press.

McLoughlin, William G. 1978. *Revivals, Awakenings, and Reform: An Essay on Religion and Social Change in America, 1607–1977.* Chicago and London: The University of Chicago Press.

Meyers, Marvin. 1960. *The Jacksonian Persuasion: Politics and Belief.* New York: Vintage Books.

Mill, John Stuart. 1963. *Essays on Politics and Culture.* Ed. by Gertrude Himmelfarb. Garden City, N.Y.: Doubleday Anchor.

———. 1958. *Nature and Utility of Religion.* New York: The Liberal Arts Press, Inc.

Miller, Joshua. 1991. *The Rise and Fall of Democracy in Early America, 1630–1789: The Legacy for Contemporary Politics*. University Park, Pennsylvania: The Pennsylvania State University Press.

Miller, Perry. 1964. *Errand Into the Wilderness*. New York: Harper Torchbooks.

Moltmann, Jurgen. 1986. Christian theology and political religion. In *Civil Religion and Political Theology*. Ed. Leroy S. Rouner, 41–58. Notre Dame: University of Notre Dame Press.

Montesquieu, Baron de. 1949a. *Oeuvres completes* [Complete works]. Ed. by Roger Callois, vol. 1: Lettres Persanes [Persian Letters] Paris: Libraire Gallimard.

———. 1949b. *The Spirit of the Laws*. Trans. Thomas Nugent. New York: Hafner Press.

Morgan, Edmund S. 1965. *Puritan Political Ideas: 1558–1794*. Indianapolis: The Bobbs-Merrill Company.

Neuhaus, Richard John. 1992. A new order of religious freedom. *First Things*. 20:13–17.

———. 1990. Polygamy, peyote, and the public peace. *First Things*. 6:63–68.

———. 1986. From civil religion to public philosophy. In *Civil Religion and Political Theology*. Ed. Leroy S. Rouner, 98–110. Notre Dame: University of Notre Dame Press.

———. 1984. *The Naked Public Square: Religion and Democracy in America*. Grand Rapids, Michigan: William B. Eerdmans Publishing Company.

Nisbet, Robert. 1975. The New Despotism. *Commentary*. 59 (6):31–43.

O'Brien, David M. 1991. *Constitutional law and politics*. Vol. 2 *Civil rights and civil liberties*. New York: W. W. Norton and Company.

Pangle, Thomas L. 1988. *The Spirit of Modern Republicanism*. Chicago and London: The University of Chicago Press.

————. 1973. *Montesquieu's Philosophy of Liberalism: A Commentary on The Spirit of the Laws.* Chicago and London: The University of Chicago Press.

Pascal, Blaise. 1941. *Pensées and The Provincial Letters.* Trans. W. F. Trotter and Thomas M'Crie. New York: Random House.

Pierson, George Wilson. 1938. *Tocqueville and Beaumont in America.* New York: Oxford University Press.

Pocock, J.G.A. 1975. *The Machiavellian Moment: Florentine Political Thought and the Atlantic Republican Tradition.* Princeton: Princeton University Press.

Richardson, William D. 1991. Racial Equality in America. In *Interpreting Tocqueville's Democracy in America.* Ed. Ken Masugi, 462–479. Savage, Maryland: Rowman and Littlefield Publishers, Inc.

Richey, Russell E. and Donald G. Jones. 1974. *American Civil Religion.* New York: Harper and Row Publishers, Inc.

Roof, Wade Clark. 1983. America's voluntary establishment: Mainline religion in transition. In *Religion and America: Spiritual Life in a Secular Age.* Eds. Mary Douglas and Steven Tipton, 130–149. Boston: Beacon Press.

Roof, Wade Clark and William McKinney. 1987. *American Mainline Religion: Its Changing Shape and Future.* New Brunswick and London: Rutgers University Press.

Rouner, Leroy S. 1986. To be at home: civil religion as common bond. In *Civil Religion and Political Theology.* Ed. Leroy S. Rouner, 125–137. Notre Dame: University of Notre Dame Press.

Rousseau, Jean Jacques. 1979. *Emile or On Education.* Trans. Allan Bloom. New York: Basic Books.

————. 1978. *On the Social Contract with Geneva Manuscript and Political Economy.* Ed. Roger D. Masters. Trans. Judith R. Masters. New York: Saint Martin's Press.

Salkever, Stephen G. 1990. *Finding the Mean: Theory and Practice in Aristotelian Political Philosophy.* Princeton: Princeton University Press.

Sandler, Gerald. 1960. "Lockean ideas in Thomas Jefferson's 'Bill for Establishing Religious Freedom.' " *Journal of the History of Ideas* 21:110–116.

Sandoz, Ellis. 1990. *A Government of Laws: Political Theory, Religion, and the American Founding.* Baton Rouge and London: Louisiana State University Press.

Schleifer, James T. 1991. Jefferson and Tocqueville. In *Interpreting Tocqueville's Democracy in America.* Ed. Ken Masugi, 178–203. Savage, Maryland: Rowman and Littlefield Publishers, Inc.

———. 1982. Tocqueville and religion: Some new perspectives. *The Tocqueville Review* 4:303–321.

———. 1980. *The Making of Tocqueville's Democracy in America.* Chapel Hill: The University of North Carolina Press.

———. 1975. "Alexis de Tocqueville describes the American character: Two previously unpublished portraits." *South Atlantic Quarterly.* 74:244–258.

Smith, Bruce James. 1991. A liberal of a new kind. In *Interpreting Tocqueville's Democracy in America.* Ed. Ken Masugi, 63–95. Savage, Maryland: Rowman and Littlefield Publishers, Inc.

Strauss, Leo. 1959. *What is Political Philosophy? and Other Studies.* Glencoe, Illinois: The Free Press.

Strout, Cushing. 1974. *The New Heavens and the New Earth: Political Religion in America.* New York: Harper and Row Publishers, Inc.

Sullivan, Andrew. 1990. "Incense and sensibility." *New Republic.* Sept. 24, 1990:33–38.

Tinder, Glenn. 1989. *The Political Meaning of Christianity: An Interpretation.* Baton Rouge and London: Louisiana State University Press.

Tipton, Steven. 1983. The moral logic of alternative religions. In *Religion and America: Spiritual Life in a Secular Age.* Eds. Mary Douglas and Steven Tipton, 79–107. Boston: Beacon Press.

Tocqueville, Alexis de. 1985. *Selected Letters on Politics and Society.* Ed. and Trans. Roger Boesche (with James Taupin). Berkeley and Los Angeles: University of California Press.

————. 1971. *Recollections.* Ed. J. P. Mayer and A. P. Kerr. Trans. George Lawrence. Garden City, N.Y.: Doubleday Anchor.

————. 1969. *Democracy in America* (Vol. 1 orig. pub., 1835; Vol. 2 orig. pub. 1840). Ed. J. P. Mayer. Trans. George Lawrence. Garden City, N.Y.: Doubleday Anchor.

————. 1960. *Journey to America.* Ed. J. P. Mayer. Trans. George Lawrence. New Haven: Yale University Press.

————. 1959. *"The European Revolution" & Correspondence with Gobineau.* Ed. and Trans. John Lukacs. Garden City, N.Y.: Doubleday Anchor.

————. 1955. *The Old Regime and the French Revolution.* Trans. Stuart Gilbert. Garden City, N.Y.: Doubleday Anchor.

————. 1951. Oeuvres Complètes. 18 vols. to date. Ed. J.P. Mayer. Paris: Gallimard.

————. 1861. *Memoirs, Letters, and Remains of Alexis de Tocqueville.* Ed. Gustave de Beaumont. Trans. by the translator of Napoleon's correspondence with King Joseph. 2 vols. Cambridge and London, England: Macmillan and Co.

————. 1860–1866. *Oeuvres Complètes.* 9 vols. Ed. Gustave de Beaumont. Paris: Michel Levy.

————. 1836. Political and social condition of France. *The London and Westminister Review.* III and XXV: 137–169.

Vaughan, Alden T. 1972. *The Puritan Tradition in America 1620–1730*. Columbia, South Carolina: University of South Carolina Press.

Wald, Kenneth D. 1987. *Religion and Politics in the United States*. New York: St. Martin's Press.

Vonnegut, Kurt Jr. 1983. Harrison Bergeron. In *Readings in American Government*. Ed. Mary P. Nichols, 516–521. Dubuque, Iowa: Kendall-Hunt.

Washington, George. 1940. *The Writings of George Washington from the Original Manuscript Sources 1745–1799*. Ed. John C. Fitzpatrick. Vol. 35. Washington: Government Printing Office.

West, Thomas G. 1991. Misunderstanding the American founding. In *Interpreting Tocqueville's Democracy in America*. Ed. Ken Masugi, 155–177. Savage, Maryland: Rowman and Littlefield Publishers, Inc.

Wilentz, Sean. 1988. Many democracies: On Tocqueville and Jacksonian America. In *Reconsidering Tocqueville's Democracy in America*. Ed. Abraham S. Eisenstadt. 207–228. New Brunswick and London: Rutgers University Press.

Wills, Garry. 1978. *Inventing America: Jefferson's Declaration of Independence*. Garden City, N.Y.: Doubleday Anchor.

Wilson, John F. 1986. Common religion in American society. In *Civil Religion and Political Theology*. Ed. Leroy S. Rouner, 111–124. Notre Dame: University of Notre Dame Press.

Winthrop, Delba. 1991. Rights: a point of honor. In *Interpreting Tocqueville's Democracy in America*. Ed. Ken Masugi, 394–424. Savage, Maryland: Rowman and Littlefield Publishers, Inc.

———. 1988. Race and freedom in Tocqueville. In *The Revival of Constitutionalism*. Ed. James W. Miller, 151–171. Lincoln and London: University of Nebraska Press.

Wood, Gordon S. 1989. "Struggle over the Puritans." *New York*

Review of Books. Nov. 9, 1989:26–34.

Wuthnow, Robert. 1988. Divided we fall: America's two civil religions. *Christian Century.* 115:395–399.

Zetterbaum, Marvin. 1967. *Tocqueville and the Problem of Democracy.* Stanford: Stanford University Press.

Zuckert, Catherine H. 1992. The role of religion in preserving American liberty—Tocqueville's analysis 150 years later. In *Liberty, Equality, and Democracy.* Ed. Eduardo Nolla, 21–36. New York and London: New York University Press.

———. 1991. Political sociology versus speculative philosophy. In *Interpreting Tocqueville's Democracy in America.* Ed. Ken Masugi, 121–152. Savage, Maryland: Rowman and Littlefield Publishers, Inc.

———. 1981. Not by preaching: Tocqueville on the role of religion in American democracy. *The Review of Politics.* 42 (April):259–280.

Zuckert, Michael P. 1986. John Locke and the problem of civil religion. In *The Moral Foundations of the American Republic.* Ed. Robert H. Horwitz, 181–203. Charlottesville: The University Press of Virginia.

INDEX